W9-BCV-186

CONTENTS

The bell-rope is pulled before prayers in a Shinto shrine.

Tokyo Tower, both a broadcasting and sight-seeing tower, is a replica of the Eiffel Tower in Paris.

JAPAN

Rex Shelley & Teo Chuu Yong & Russell Mok

MARSHALL CAVENDISH BENCHMARK

NEW YORK

PICTURE CREDITS

ANA Press Agency, Axiom Photographic Agency, Bes Stock, Sheila Brown, Jon Burbank, Getty Images / Hulton Archive, Haga Library, The Hutchison Library, Jimmy Kang, Peter Korn, Lonely Planet Images, Harold Pfeiffer, Photobank Photo Library, Luca I. Tettoni, Yoshinoya Pte Ltd

PRECEDING PAGE

Children dressed in traditional summer attire walk through a rice field in Aichi Prefecture during the Tanabata Festival. The children are carrying bamboo branches decorated with poems written on colorful paper strips.

Marshall Cavendish Benchmark
99 White Plains Road
Tarrytown, NY 10591
Website: www.marshallcavendish.us

© Times Media Private Limited 1990, 2002
© Marshall Cavendish International (Asia) Private Limited 2004
All rights reserved. First edition 1990. Second edition 2002.
® "Cultures of the World" is a registered trademark of Times Publishing Limited.

Originated and designed by Times Editions
An imprint of Marshall Cavendish International (Asia) Private Limited
A member of Times Publishing Limited

All Internet sites were correct and accurate at the time of printing.

Library of Congress Cataloging-in-Publication Data
Shelley, Rex, 1930–
   Japan / Rex Shelley.
      p. cm. — (Cultures of the world)
   Includes bibliographical references and index.
   ISBN 0-7614-1356-1
   1. Japan—Juvenile literature [1. Japan.] I. Title. II. Series.
   DS806 .S45 2001
   952—dc21   2001028609

Printed in Malaysia

INTRODUCTION

IN AUGUST 1945 battle-weary Japan surrendered to the Allied powers. For more than six years after its surrender, Japan was placed under Allied, mainly American, control to undergo social and political reforms. In 1951 Japan signed the San Francisco Peace Treaty, which allowed its return to the community of nations as a reformed state.

Japan's primary task during the postwar years was economic rehabilitation. By the mid-1960s Japan had become an industrialized nation, able to compete successfully in the open markets of the world. The Tokyo Olympics of 1964 symbolized the new confidence of the Japanese people and the country's increasing stature in the international community. Today, Japanese brand names like Sony, Toyota, Seiko, Panasonic, and Honda are well known throughout the world and are synonymous with corporate ingenuity and successful globalization.

GEOGRAPHY

JAPAN LIES between longitudes 122° and 148° east in the North Pacific Ocean. The Japanese name of the country, *Nippon*, means sun's origin, because the Japanese once believed that the sun first shone on Japan. The country is also known as the Land of the Rising Sun.

Japan consists of 4,000 mountainous islands in a bow-shaped cluster. The four largest islands, Hokkaido, Honshu, Kyushu, and Shikoku, form the core of Japan, and of these, Honshu, the central and largest island, is the living heart. In the past, imperial and feudal powers were concentrated on Honshu. Today, the island is the industrial hub of modern Japan and home to almost 80 percent of the population. The highest mountain (Mount Fuji, 12,389 feet/3,776 m), the longest river (Shinano, 228 miles/367 km), and the largest lake (Biwa) are all on Honshu.

South of Honshu is Shikoku, the smallest of the four major islands. Although close to Honshu, Shikoku has been a rustic appendage to the mainstream of activity and development. At the southwest end of Honshu lies the island of Kyushu. It has a subtropical climate and, in a way, is the "sunshine state" of Japan. It is the island nearest to Korea and to the cultural influences of China. To the north of Honshu lies the large island of Hokkaido, the Alaska of Japan, with bitterly cold winters and harsh volcanic mountains. It was once an island for outcasts.

Japan can also be called the land of volcanoes. Violent eruptions occur frequently, and it is believed that at least 80 volcanoes have been active since the beginning of Japan's history. New volcanoes born in this century include Showa-shinzan on Hokkaido and Myojin-sho off the Bayonnaise Rocks in the Pacific. Japan's well-known landmark, Mount Fuji, is also a volcano. As a result of volcanic activity, especially in the northeast and southwest, crater-like depressions called calderas are prevalent, though most are now filled with water, forming lakes.

Opposite: **Two waterfalls in Nikko, north of Tokyo. Nikko is a popular spot for viewing autumn foliage in Japan.**

The symmetrical and serene Mount Fuji.

A LAND OF MOUNTAINS

Japan was once part of the great Asian continent. Sometime during the Ice Age, the Asian land mass broke up and the peaks of the old continent became the 4,000 islands of Japan. The average elevation of the four main islands is 1,000 feet (305 m). The Pacific Ocean to the east and south and the Sea of Japan between Japan and China did not erode the land and change it significantly.

Neither did the volcanoes, although Japan lies at the confluence of two volcanic belts that ring a large part of the Pacific. There are about 67 "live" volcanoes, that is, volcanoes that are either active or potentially active. Mount Fuji, Japan's highest mountain, is a dormant volcano. The Japanese call it "Fuji-san" (*san* means mountain). This mountain is the spiritual symbol of Japan.

About 72 percent of Japan is mountainous and too steep for development. This steep terrain has meant that many Japanese traditionally made their living with ships and fishing. Every major city is located near the sea.

As island people do everywhere, the Japanese turned to the sea for their sustenance and dreams. But the mountains are always in the background, helping to shape the Japanese character, teaching stoic resilience. Because of volcanic eruptions, the Japanese had to fashion their buildings to withstand upheavals. Using the products of mountain forests, they built timber and straw houses that kept them cool in hot summers but could not insulate them against the harsh winter cold. These traditional houses have nearly all disappeared.

EARTHQUAKES

On September 1, 1923, the greatest earthquake in Japan's history shook the western part of Honshu around the city of Tokyo. The death toll from the earthquake was about 100,000. Tokyo was flattened, but within four years modern Tokyo had risen from the ruins. More recently, the Great Hanshin-Awaji earthquake shook the Kobe/Osaka region on January 17, 1995.

Earthquakes are a constant danger in Japan. If they occur near the

Members of the Young Men's Association of Japan, who were among the first to reach the scene after the catastrophic earthquake of 1923, carrying an elderly woman out of the danger zone.

surface, the damage can be tremendous. If they occur along the ocean floor, they generate *tsunami* ("tsoo-nah-mee"), high tidal waves capable of wiping out coastal areas.

A 50-foot (15-m) high *torii* ("toh-ree-ee"), or gate leading to a Shinto shrine, rises out of the sea off the island of Miyajima near Hiroshima, welcoming the gods of the sea to the island.

RIVERS AND LAKES

The rain- and snow-fed rivers of Japan are small and swift, many of them hurtling like waterfalls to the sea. There are numerous lakes. Lakes have always held a great fascination for the Japanese. It is probably the lake as a calm inland sea that attracts these island and mountain people spiritually—the unexpectedness of calm, still water appearing in the ruggedness of the mountains. Lake Biwa, located on Honshu, is Japan's largest and most beautiful lake. It is revered by the Japanese for its historical and cultural significance.

CLIMATE

If it were not for three major factors, Japan, as an island-nation, would enjoy a mild and pleasant temperate climate. These factors are the large air mass over Siberia; the warm, moist air blowing in from the Pacific; and, cutting across these air currents, the mountain ranges that run perpendicular to the direction of the winds.

During the winter months, December to February, Siberia's high pressure areas periodically cause waves of cold air to flow south, lowering the temperature throughout Japan. As the winds from central Siberia cross the Sea of Japan, they meet warm air currents flowing northward, absorb large amounts of moisture, and deposit it as snow in the mountains. As a result, Japan has one of the heaviest annual snowfalls in the world.

During the summer months, June to August, the weather is influenced by the high pressure areas in the Pacific Ocean and the low pressure areas over Siberia. The airstreams flow north and east, bringing heat and moisture. Tokyo and Osaka, in particular, are unbearably hot and humid at this time. The highest temperature ever recorded in Tokyo is 102° F (39° C).

The winds change in spring and fall making them the most pleasant times in Japan.

"PLUM RAINS" AND TYPHOONS

In early summer, cold currents of air flowing from the north meet moist currents from the South Pacific and produce periods of rainy weather. Rains can be intense at times, causing floods and crop damage, but these early summer rains make it possible to grow rice in Japan. The Japanese call them *tsuyu*—the direct translation of the Chinese characters is "plum rains"—and write poetry about them.

At the end of the summer, Japan is subjected to typhoons blowing in from the Pacific. These winds can reach speeds of 130 miles (209 km) per hour. Like hurricanes, typhoons cause damage, but they also bring rain.

VEGETATION

Japan's climate, ranging from subtropical to temperate and cold, encourages the growth of a great variety of trees. Mangrove swamps are found in the coastal regions of the southern Ryukyus, while in Kyushu, Shikoku, and southern Honshu, evergreens flourish. Mountain forests in central and northern Honshu are rich with broadleaf deciduous trees such as maple, ash, birch, beech, and poplar. Evergreens there include fir, spruce, larch, hemlock, and Japanese cedar. Pines and the white beech grow in Hokkaido. From spring to fall, Japanese forests are a spectacular sight.

RANDOM FACTS ABOUT JAPAN'S ANIMAL LIFE

Native primate: Japanese macaque
Largest snake: Japanese rat snake, 5 feet (1.50 m) long and harmless
Famous amphibian*:* A species of giant salamander of the *Cryptobranchidae* family, which lives in Kyushu and western Honshu. It is one of the largest living amphibians, reaching 5 feet (1.50 m) in length
Notorious insect*:* The Japanese beetle, which was accidentally imported into the Americas in 1916. A swarm of Japanese beetles can strip a peach tree in 15 minutes, leaving only branches and pits.

The Japanese beetle.

HISTORY

SCHOLARS DIFFER ABOUT early Japanese history as there is limited data. Important sources of information are two chronicles written in the eighth century, the *Kojiki (Records of Ancient Matters,* A.D. 712) and the *Nihon Shoki (Written Chronicle of Japan,* A.D. 720). Both describe an elaborate mythology.

The early Japanese, a Mongoloid race, were migrants from China, Korea, and Manchuria who came across the Tsushima Strait to southwestern Honshu (some believe at Izumo) and Kyushu. Scholars have suggested that migrants may also have included people of Malay stock from Oceania, the islands of the Pacific. Japan's early inhabitants were hunter-gatherers. Around 200 B.C., a new agricultural society developed.

The early settlers found a strange and uncivilized aboriginal people, the Ainu, a Neolithic people who looked more Caucasoid than Mongoloid, with hairy skin and round eyes. The migrants from the Asian continent slowly penetrated the whole country, pushing the Ainu northward.

Opposite: **Japan was once home to thousands of castles. Inuyama Castle is one of a handful of castles that remain.**

THE FIRST JAPANESE EMPEROR

Japan's early history was marked by contact with China. It was a time riddled with struggles for power and territory. In the seventh century, one strong man emerged: Jimmu Tenno, leader of the Yamato clan and first emperor of the Imperial line.

According to mythology, Japanese emperors are descendants of the sun goddess. The first emperor was given three sacred treasures: a bronze mirror, a sword, and a bead (in another version, this is a string of precious stones). With these treasures, he convinced the warring clans of his divine descent. His empire became a powerful one, centered in Nara. Only the melted bronze mirror remains, at the Grand Shrine of Ise (see page 71).

Japanese sculpture was refined in the Heian period and reached its peak in the Kamakura period. On the right is an example of Kamakura sculpture housed in the Todaiji temple in Nara.

HEIAN, A GOLDEN AGE

Japan enjoyed relative peace from A.D. 794 to 1185. The capital was moved from Nara to Heian-kyo, meaning the capital of peace and calm, hence the Heian period. Heian-kyo was later called Kyoto, simply meaning capital. The Japanese *kana* ("kah-nah") scripts were created and the arts flourished. The classic novel, *The Tale of Genji,* was written by Murasaki Shikibu in A.D. 1000, revealing many details of court life.

SHOGUN AND SAMURAI

While culture flourished, the poverty of the general population provoked uprisings. Out of the battles to suppress these rebellions, Minamoto Yoritomo emerged as the most powerful warrior. He challenged the emperor's authority and the ultimate power passed from the Imperial court and its aristocracy in Kyoto to the military lord, the *shogun* ("show-goon").

Minamoto Yoritomo (the Japanese put their family name before their given name) established his seat of government at Kamakura in 1185. In 1192, he was given the title of *shogun*. It was during the period of the Kamakura shogunate (a dynasty of *shogun*) that the ethical code of the *samurai* ("sah-moo-rye"), or Japanese warrior, was developed. Japan was then a feudal society and the *samurai* were the armed champions of the leading families.

ASHIKAGA SHOGUNATE In 1333, the Kamakura shogunate fell and the Ashikaga family took over the shogunate in 1338. Their regime, which lasted until 1573, was racked with rivalry and other troubles. The mountainous terrain made central control difficult, and the country was split into warring states. Regional self-sufficiency became important, and localized industry, transportation facilities, and public works projects were developed.

A *daimyo* ("dye-mee-yoh"), or feudal lord, never traveled without his *samurai* ("sah-moo-rye"), or trusted warrior.

"The strong manly ones in life are those who understand the meaning of the word patience.*"*

—*Tokugawa Ieyasu*

UNIFICATION

The 16th century was a time of major events. Three great men, Oda Nobunaga, Toyotomi Hideyoshi, and Tokugawa Ieyasu, unified the country and set the stage for the dawning of modern Japan.

Oda Nobunaga (1534–82) overpowered his rivals by the use of crude muskets that were being made in central Japan. By 1568 he was the strongest figure and set himself the task of uniting Japan under the control of a single powerful authority. He succeeded in uniting about half the country in the area around Kyoto.

Toyotomi Hideyoshi (1536–98), one of Oda Nobunaga's generals, succeeded him. He was an unattractive man, almost a dwarf, but with a charisma that was both powerful and dynamic. His leadership was marked by the development of several institutions, including a new system of taxation to fund his invasion of Korea (which failed) and the growth of mercantile centers. Japan enjoyed prosperity and stability under Hideyoshi.

Tokugawa Ieyasu (1542–1616), who succeeded Hideyoshi, established his position at the battle of Sekigahara in 1600. By 1603, Ieyasu had been given the title of *shogun*. This cool, unshakeable man of iron spent forty years fighting and developed into a high-caliber military commander as well as a faultless judge of character. The Tokugawa firmly ruled Japan for more than 250 years.

WESTERN INFLUENCE

The success of these three military strategists has to be seen against the background of Western influence. In mid-16th century, the first ships from the West arrived in Japan, bringing Christian missionaries who made rapid progress converting the populace. The Westerners also brought with them the smooth bore musket, which changed the strategies of feudal battles.

Along with the flow of the Portuguese and Dutch missionaries and traders into southern Japan came an Englishman, Will Adams. Adams eventually became a trusted adviser to Ieyasu. The town of Ito holds an annual festival in his honor, and there are several monuments to this Westerner in a number of places in Japan.

The Christians brought with them many problems, not the least of which was the rivalry among the different Christian groups. They also stirred up new loyalties among the Japanese converts. The conflicts finally erupted in a siege of Shimabara in Kyushu (1637–38). No help arrived for the Christian insurgents and they were all killed.

The *daimyo* were kept constantly on the move to prevent them from consolidating power in their own territory. They were obliged to leave their families permanently in Edo (old Tokyo), the seat of power. They were themselves required to live alternate years in their own territories and in Edo. Above is an artist's rendition of a typical *daimyo* procession to Edo. The route and the number of attendants were decided on by the *shogun*.

Below: **Arrival of Commodore Perry in Edo (old Tokyo).**

Opposite top: **German Dr. Erwin Bälz, who was one of many foreign advisers in Japan, lectured at Tokyo Imperial University for 26 years. He and another German, Julius Scriba, are known as the fathers of Japanese medicine.**

Opposite bottom: **An early Japanese mission (1871) sent overseas to study the conditions and customs in the West.**

ISOLATION AND THE WESTERN "INVASION"

The Tokugawa shogunate threw out all foreigners and closed the country to the world in 1637. No Japanese were allowed to travel out of Japan, and to make this edict effective, there was a restriction on the size of boats that could be constructed. For the next 200 years Japan was isolated from the world. Only the Dutch were permitted a small trading station at Nagasaki.

The Europeans and the American pioneers who were building their trading empires, however, had other ideas. In Russia, groups of financiers and traders with their eye on the profits Japan could yield managed to persuade their reluctant government to send a fleet to Japan. Admiral Putyatin arrived in Nagasaki in August 1853, hoping to reverse Japan's isolationist policy. He was preceded by an American, Commodore Matthew C. Perry, who had sailed into Tokyo harbor on July 8, 1853, with four warships, two of them powered by steam. The Americans wanted to open diplomatic and trade relations, and they needed bases for their China trade and coal for their steamships.

The Japanese rulers were startled and shaken by the American demands. At the same time, from reports that trickled in through the Dutch, they realized that they were defenseless against the new military technology of the West. Making a painful but realistic decision, they made some concessions. Diplomatic relations were established and the United States given trading rights at two ports.

TRANSFORMATION

Japan entered into a period of intense learning about all things Western. By the selective absorption of Western ideas and technology over the ensuing 50 years, Japan developed into a modern industrial nation.

The Japanese examined and sifted the new concepts and technologies, not through the usual process of human contact, but by close study of books and objects. Perhaps this is why the country emerged from the modernizing process with its inner soul Japanese. It also explains why today the *gaijin* ("guy-jin"), meaning foreigners, find the Japanese so much like themselves, yet so different at their core.

MEIJI RESTORATION In 1867, the Emperor Komei died and his 15-year-old son took over as the Emperor Meiji. He was to rule Japan for 45 years, during its great golden era of growth and modernization. In the following year, 1868, the great house of Tokugawa, which had provided Japan with 15 *shogun*, collapsed. Power went to the imperial throne.

The imperial family did not cling to its new-found power. In the spirit of the changing times, a constitution was written in 1889 and the Imperial Diet, the governing body of Japan, was set up in 1890. These were the first steps toward the full democracy attained in 1946, under a new post-war constitution.

MILITARY MIGHT

In the eighty-seven years between 1854, when America forced Japan to end its isolation, and the start of the war in the Pacific in 1941, Japan built up a fighting force. In 1894 Japan fought China over control of Korea. To the world's surprise, Japan defeated China, gaining Taiwan, parts of China and Korean independence. Much to Japan's resentment, Russia, France, and Germany forced Japan to return the Chinese territory. The Emperor Meiji met the massive popular indignation with a plea that they should try "to bear the unbearable." In 1945, when Japan surrendered at the end of World War II, Emperor Hirohito used the same words.

Another battle, the battle of the Sea of Japan against the Russian fleet during the Russo-Japanese War in 1905, had a greater historical impact than the war with China. In two days, the Japanese destroyed the Russian Baltic fleet of forty vessels. It was the first major victory of an Asian nation against a Western one and established Japan as a world power. It destroyed the myth of Western invulnerability and had an energizing effect on the morale of Asian nationalists in colonized territories.

A Japanese general accepts surrender from a Russian commander during the Russo-Japanese War.

In Japan, there was a struggle between the militarists, who wanted war, and the moderates, who did not. However, charged with confidence from the Russo-Japanese War, the militaristic elements in the country gained strength and adopted an expansionist policy. In 1910 Japan annexed Korea, ruling it for the next thirty-five years, and in 1931 Japan occupied Manchuria, then expanded into Inner Mongolia and parts of China. By 1936 Japanese millitary leaders controlled the Japanese government.

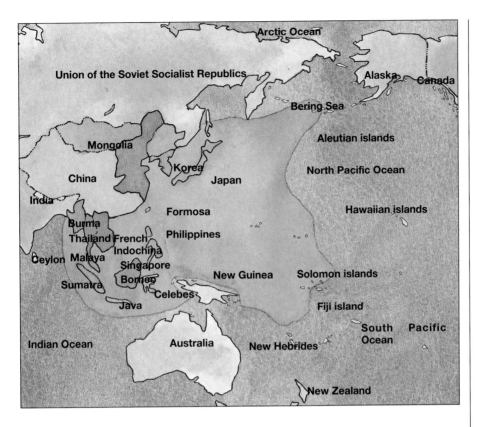

THE WAR IN THE PACIFIC

World War II began in Europe in 1939. Meanwhile Japan continued its expansion in Asia and signed an agreement with Germany and Italy. In July 1941 Japanese troops moved into Vietnam. The United States, Britain, and Holland responded with an economic embargo of Japan. Talks between the United States and Japan failed in November 1941, and a Japanese fleet assembled in the Kurile Islands northeast of Hokkaido set sail for the North Pacific. At dawn on December 7, 1941, Japanese planes bombed the US Pacific fleet anchored at Pearl Harbor in Hawaii, crippling the US fleet in the surprise attack.

The Japanese army swept quickly through Southeast Asia and the Pacific islands. Hong Kong, Burma, Thailand, Malaya, Indonesia, and the Philippines fell to Japanese control.

The Japanese empire in 1942 covered all of Southeast Asia.

The atomic-bombed cities of Hiroshima and Nagasaki were built up rapidly after the Pacific War, but the ruins of one building were left as a memorial. It is known as the Atomic Bomb Dome in Hiroshima.

WORLD WAR II ENDS

The Battle of Midway, fought between the Japanese navy and the Allied forces in June 1942, in which the Japanese were beaten, was the turning point of the war in the Pacific. In the next three years Japan lost a series of battles. In February 1945 American forces landed on Iwo Jima. The Japanese fought to the last man. The area of Iwo Jima is 8 square miles (21 square km), and capturing it cost 7,000 American lives. The Japanese fought with the same ferocity through April, May, and June on Okinawa. Almost 200,000 soldiers and civilians lost their lives.

At 8:15 A.M. on August 6, 1945, an American Superfortress dropped an atomic bomb on Hiroshima. Russia declared war on Japan on August 8. A second atomic bomb was dropped on Nagasaki on August 9. On August 13 over 1,500 planes bombarded Tokyo. On August 14 American aircraft dropped thousands of leaflets over Tokyo, giving the Japanese the details of messages exchanged between the Allies and the Japanese government. Emperor Hirohito announced Japan's surrender on August 14, 1945.

KAMIKAZE

In 1274 and 1281 the Mongol conqueror Kublai Khan attempted to conquer Japan, but failed because typhoons destroyed his ships.

The Japanese regarded the typhoon as a divine intervention and called it *kamikaze* ("kah-mee-kah-zay"), wind of the gods. During World War II, they applied this name to their force of suicide pilots. This painting shows university students joining the *Kamikaze*.

THE OCCUPATION

The seven years of American occupation that followed, under US General Douglas MacArthur, prepared the ground for an economic revival. For the second time in a hundred years, Japan underwent a transformation, from a war-torn country to one of the major industrial nations in the world.

Japan was rebuilt along the lines of the Western world, but it was not a wholesale enforcement of Western models. There was careful selection of what could be changed. There were misjudgments, too, as when the occupation administration tried to dissolve the powerful monopolistic *zaibatsu* ("zye-baht-soo"), which literally means economic group, but altogether the changes helped to set the foundations of postwar Japan in areas such as the constitution, the legal system, and language.

GOVERNMENT

JAPAN IS a democracy with a titular monarch, the emperor. As in the United Kingdom, the monarch has no legal powers but commands great respect and is symbolically the head of the nation.

The imperial family of Japan descends from an unbroken lineage of nearly 2,000 years. No other royal family in history has held its position for so long. The origins of the imperial family are obscure and mixed with myth, but historians generally agree that the first emperor ruled around the time of Christ. The family laid claim to divine origin and held a role of religious leadership, but these were renounced on New Year's Day, 1946.

The imperial family survived the power struggles of feudal Japan because the military men who controlled the land always kept the emperor as the symbolic head of their nation. Throughout the centuries, the family has been a quiet and stabilizing influence on Japan.

Opposite: **Emperor Akihito and Empress Michiko. On his ascension to the throne on January 7, 1989, the era of the new emperor was designated Heisei ("Peace and Concord").**

Above: **The imperial crest. In ancient times the family crest helped warriors to tell friend from foe during hand-to-hand combat.**

Left: **Newlyweds Crown Prince Naruhito and Crown Princess Masako in traditional wedding robes.**

DEMOCRACY AND THE GOVERNMENT

Japan was the first Asian country to introduce a parliamentary system. The first constitution, introduced in 1885, did not give power to the people; the emperor still had ultimate control. However, it did lay the foundation for future democracy. Today, Japan is administered under a constitution that was completely redrafted by the American administration in 1947. Japan's second constitution retained the monarchy but subjected it to the will of the people.

Ito Hirobumi, who was sent to Europe in order to draft a constitution. In 1885, the government adopted a cabinet system and Ito Hirobumi became the first prime minister of Japan.

The Japanese parliament, called the Diet, is made up of two chambers. The 480 members of the House of Representatives serve a term of four years. The 252 members of the House of Councillors serve a six-year term. In practice, general elections take place every two years. The House of Councillors has weaker powers than the House of Representatives; vetoes by councillors can be overturned by a simple majority vote of representatives, but not vice versa. The chief executive is the prime minister, who is elected by the Diet and is usually the head of the majority party.

Amid rising unemployment and the most severe economic recession of the postwar period, Koizumi Junichiro became prime minister of Japan in May, 2001. Koizumi's Cabinet includes four women. Tanaka Makiko, daughter of former prime minister Tanaka Kakuei, is the first woman in Japanese history to become Minister of Foreign Affairs.

Japan is divided into 47 districts called prefectures. There are city, town, and village assemblies for local administration.

The Diet in session.

MAJOR POLITICAL PARTIES

Party	Representatives	Councillors
Liberal Democratic Party	233	105
Democratic Party of Japan	127	56
New Komeito	31	0
Liberal Party	22	12
Japan Communist Party	20	23
Social Democratic Party	19	14
Komeito	0	24
New Conservative Party	7	0
Mushozoku-no-kai (Unaffiliated Group)	5	10
Liberal League	1	4
Independents	15	4
TOTAL	480	252

(As of January 2001)

THE LEGAL SCENE

The Supreme Court is in principle a body to counterbalance the powers of the Diet and the Cabinet. The chief justice and 14 associate justices of the Supreme Court are, however, appointed by the Cabinet for life terms (they retire at age 70). There has never been any major confrontation among these three centers of power. Under the Supreme Court there are eight High Courts and below these the district courts, one for each prefecture except Hokkaido, which has four.

Japanese law is framed in written codes, introduced in the 19th century, that are referred to but not upheld rigidly. There is no jury system and the procedure in a Japanese courtroom is more subdued and less dramatic than that of a typical American or European one. The low level of litigation in Japan is reflected in the fact that there is one lawyer to every 9,000 people in Japan, compared to the United States, for instance, where the ratio is one lawyer to 400 people.

There are no legal enforcement treaties with other countries. If there were a legal dispute between, say, a Canadian and a Japanese on a contract written under Canadian law, the Canadian would not be able to enforce it unless the Japanese party had assets in Canada.

Bright yellow caps of schoolchildren alert drivers to children crossing roads. It is a practice to place a bin of yellow plastic flags on either side of a pedestrian crossing. The pedestrian stretches out the flag horizontally in front of him while crossing, then places it in the bin on the other side.

DEFENSE

The 1947 Constitution included a "no-war" clause (Article 9), one of the requirements of the MacArthur administration. The army and navy were abolished. In 1951 Japan and the United States signed a security treaty. In

1953 US vice-president Richard Nixon, speaking in Tokyo, stated that his country had been wrong to include Article 9 in the Japanese constitution.

In 1954 Self-Defense Forces were set up with the Police Reserve Force as a base. Today there are 149,000 men and 46,000 reserves in their ground force, 43,000 in the air force and 44,000 in the navy. Until 1986 Japan had limited its defense expenditure to about 1 percent of its gross national product (GNP), but since its GNP is very high, the sum is substantial.

THE POLICE

Japan has a large police force—about one officer per 495 people—and has one of the lowest crime rates in the world. However, small extremist groups that oppose the law exist.

The Japanese Self-Defense Forces (SDF) is active in providing relief assistance to war and disaster-stricken countries.

ECONOMY

JAPAN'S current economy grew out of the rubble of World War II, which ended in 1945. Forty-one years later, in 1986, the per capita income of Japan overtook that of the United States of America to become the highest in the world.

In the 1980s, Japanese multinational corporations built factories all over the world. Japanese brands like Mitsubishi, Sanyo, and Aiwa are household names across the globe. This achievement is all the more remarkable considering Japan has no oil or mineral resources and must import most of its raw materials.

In the early 1990s, Japan began to experience an economic slowdown brought about by excessive investment in the late 1980s. In Japan the economic downturn that took place during this time is referred to as the "bursting" of the "bubble economy." In the year 2001 Japan faced its worst economic recession since the end of World War II. Experts point to the extreme rigidity of the banking system and corporate structures as one cause of the recession. In addition, an aging population and low birth rates are two major social and economic concerns as Japan lacks an adequate social welfare system.

Opposite: **Ginza, the "center of the center" of Tokyo city, is the Rodeo Drive of Japan.**

Above: **Young Japanese women enjoy wine tasting at a wine bar in Tokyo. In recent years, Japan has experienced a "wine boom," with an increasing number of Japanese obtaining professional sommelier licenses.**

THE JAPANESE WORKER

The Japanese are quick to pick up good ideas, examine them, improve on them, then remarket them. Their style is to imitate and innovate. The English invented the pocket calculator, but the Japanese flooded the market with better, more sophisticated models. The French invented a train that ran at 125 miles per hour on an air cushion, but the Japanese went one better: a train that would travel at a speed of 185 miles per hour with magnetic levitation.

Japanese industries have overtaken the world in marketing technologically new products partly because of industrial strategies and partly because of the discipline and full commitment of their workers. Most workers believe that the company is more important than the individual worker, and the common goal of more profits for the company is the base on which disputes are resolved. Given this attitude, it is not surprising that there are no major trade union disputes; certainly nothing like the labor-management disputes often seen in the United States and the United Kingdom.

The working population represents a larger proportion of the total population than in most Western countries. The proportion of working women is also high. About 61 percent of working women are in the service industries.

Behind the efficiency of the Japanese workers is the fact that they have a very high average level of education. About 95 percent of the Japanese continue their education beyond the compulsory basic nine years of school.

Japan's economic success has, ironically, brought on economic and political problems. Many countries view the Japanese with suspicion, regarding them (and treating them) as intruders with their export products

and their overseas manufacturing. Fortunately, Japanese workers have a resilience and self-control born out of a history of struggles against natural calamities such as earthquakes and typhoons. This, and their inclination to look for a compromise, out of reasonableness and respect for the opinions of others, should ensure that Japan retains its economic strength for many more years.

Sorting out the ayu fish. Fish is an important part of the Japanese diet, and fishing ports can be found all along the coasts of the Japanese islands.

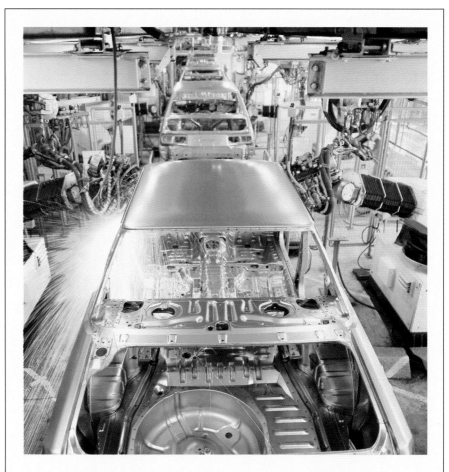

Japan is one of the world's leading producers of automobiles. In recent years, some Japanese automobile factories have started to use robots on the assembly line.

EXPORT PLANS FOR JAPANESE CARS IN 2000

Toyota Motor	1,570,000
Nissan Motor	(not available)
Mazda Motor	515,000
Honda Motor	520,000
Mitsubishi Motors	380,000
Suzuki Motor	270,000
Isuzu Motors	200,000
Fuji Heavy Industries	176,000
Daihatsu Motor	99,000
Hino Motors	15,000
Nissan Diesel Motor	12,000

KEY ECONOMIC FACTS

- 37 percent of the gross domestic product comes from manufacturing.
- Unemployment was only 4.6 percent in January 2000.
- Inflation estimated to be at -0.3 percent in 2001
- The labor pool of 68 million is a bigger proportion of total population than in any Western country.
- Japan is deficient in raw materials and relies heavily on imports.
- Japan is the world's largest importer of coal, natural gas, and oil.
- Japan is the world's largest net importer of timber.
- Although Japan produces 70 percent of the food it requires, it has been the world's largest importer of fish since 1978.

TRADE*

Major Exports
Automobiles
Iron and steel
Video cassette recorders
Office equipment
Scientific and optical equipment
Ships
Prime movers
Metal products
Radio receivers
Metalworking machinery

Major Imports
Food
Raw materials
Mineral fuels
Chemicals
Textiles
Machinery and equipment

The information here is based on 1999 data. The United States is Japan's largest trading partner, supplying about 22 percent of its imports and taking about 31 percent of Japan's exports in 1999.

ENVIRONMENT

JAPAN IS A highly industrialized nation. Some well-known Japanese products include heavy machinery and factory equipment; metals and metal products for use in construction and manufacturing; electronic equipment such as television sets, radios, cameras, and home appliances; textiles; automobiles; and chemicals. Japan, however, possesses no significant energy or mineral deposits. The country must import most of its energy supplies, primarily from the Middle East, and is one of the most efficient users of energy among the world's advanced industrial nations.

Below: **This park in Edogawa, Tokyo, makes use of recycled water to create waterfalls and other attractions.**

Nevertheless, Japan, like other industrial nations, produces pollutants that contribute to the depletion of the ozone layer and global warming.

The Japanese government set up the National Environment Agency to restrict pollution of the environment caused by Japan's industrial growth in the 1950s and 1960s and to preserve the remaining natural environment. To date, Japan has some of the strictest environmental regulations of any industrialized nation, and the quality of Japan's environment has improved in recent decades. Public interest in the environment in Japan has also increased in recent years.

Opposite: **Japan is endowed with beautiful forests, such as this cypress forest in Kitayama, Kyoto. The Japanese government has set aside many forests as conservation sites.**

39

In an effort to cut down air pollution, Japanese factories like this one are obligated by law to process exhaust gases in special machinery before releasing the gases as smoke through factory chimneys.

POLLUTION

Japan's first major encounter with pollution took place at the end of the 19th century, when runoff from the Ashio copper mine in Tochigi Prefecture polluted nearby rivers and fields, poisoning not just fish and crops but also area residents.

Pollution became widespread during the period of high-paced industrial growth that began in 1955. From the mid-1960s onward, Japan suffered serious air, water, soil, and noise pollution. People who lived near factories that burn oil or coal, like chemical plants, steelworks, and electric power plants, developed respiratory ailments. Bronchitis and asthma affected those living near the industrial complex in Yokkaichi, Mie Prefecture.

Another example of factory waste pollution was the mercury poisoning in the city of Minamata, Kumamoto Prefecture. At first the source of the poisoning was unknown, and the ailments that people developed were referred to simply as Minamata disease. Scientists eventually discovered that mercury discharged by a factory had been leaking into Minamata Bay. People who ate the contaminated fish and shellfish from the area developed numbness and other disorders of the central nervous system.

NATURE CONSERVATION

Conservation policy is handled by several government bodies. The Environment Agency, through its Nature Conservation Bureau, is responsible for conservation policy. It also manages national parks, wilderness areas, and nature conservation areas. The Ministry of Agriculture, Forestry, and Fisheries administers forest reserves and forests considered important for soil and water conservation purposes, and for their scenic beauty. The Agency for Cultural Affairs provides protection by designating certain plants, animals, or landscapes as "natural monuments." The main legislation on conservation is the Nature Conservation Law of 1972.

In Japan there are 28 national parks, which are designated and administered by the Environment Agency, and 55 quasi-national parks, which are designated and administered by the local government. Kushiro Marsh in Hokkaido and Lake Biwa in Shiga Prefecture, which are famous waterfowl habitats, have been designated as special protection districts. Several locations in the country are on the World Heritage List of natural properties, including the Shirakami mountain range in the Tohoku region and the island of Yakushima in Kagoshima Prefecture.

Hot springs are very popular with the Japanese, who enjoy the relaxing and healing effects of its waters on both the mind and body. Beppu Onsen in Kyushu is the biggest and most famous hot spring resort in Japan.

41

Garbage is carefully categorized in Japan, where trash cans in the home and in public places are clearly marked. Trash is either burned or processed for recycling.

WASTE MANAGEMENT

Garbage disposal in Japan is a serious problem. Households and offices produce approximately 2 pounds (1kg) of trash per person each day, and the mountain of garbage seems to be growing every year. Waste produced by factories and at construction sites also continues to rise, and there is a shortage of available land for landfill areas where waste can be buried between layers of earth to build up low-lying land.

Japan's primary concern in waste management is to limit the volume of garbage to be disposed of in landfill. About 75 percent of municipal solid waste is incinerated, reducing the volume of material to be disposed of in landfill by 95 percent. Unfortunately, incinerating solid waste pollutes the air. Guidelines have been developed for pollutants emitted by incinerators. As a consequence, over 70 percent of Japan's incinerators are modern, continuous combustion facilities to which the strictest guidelines apply.

RECYCLING

The government and civic groups are promoting recycling, and the amount of newspapers and beverage cans that are recycled in Japan is reaching high levels.

Recycling is now being carried out on a full scale in Japan for steel cans, aluminum cans, and glass bottles. According to statistics for 1999, 83 percent of steel cans were recycled, as were 79 percent of aluminum cans, and 79 percent of glass bottles. Also, 54 percent (as of 1997) of newspapers and other used paper were recycled. Recycling of plastic bottles has also started, but the 21,361 tons of PET (polyethylene terephthalate) bottles that were recycled in 1999 were only 23 percent of the total consumed. (PET is the type of plastic commonly used for clear plastic bottles that hold mineral water and other soft drinks.)

The 1991 Law Concerning the Promotion of the Use of Recyclable Resources sets even higher targets for the recycling of paper, glass, and other materials.

Beverage cans are collected separately, compacted in special machines, and used as raw material for new cans.

ENVIRONMENTAL PROGRAMS AND INITIATIVES

Japan has in place laws to encourage and promote good environmental practices and several select committees to work on environmental issues.

Since October 1990 Japan has had a national climate change program for the period 1991 to 2010. This program outlines a wide range of actions to be taken by both the government and the private sector to reduce the emission of greenhouse gases and to foster international cooperation on environmental issues.

In November 1993 the Japanese Diet enacted the "Basic Environment Law," which provides the legal framework for coping with global warming and other environmental problems. The measures required include surveys and research related to economic measures, as well as provisions for international cooperation on global environmental protection.

Yumenoshima Park in Tokyo is built on a landfill.

Fuel efficiency targets for the year 2000 were set higher than 1992 on average. As a result, freight transportation began shifting again toward railway and coastal shipping because of interest-free loans and special taxation measures. Increased use of public transportation was promoted, as was the development of transportation systems that generate less carbon dioxide, such as monorails and high-speed rail.

Each year, Japan provides support to environmental protection projects around the world through its international aid programs and non-governmental organizations. As demonstrated by its role as host of the December 1997 Conference on Global Climate Change in Kyoto, Japan plays a leading role in the area of climate change and cooperates closely with the United States on a number of environmental issues.

The Japanese government encourages domestic transportation of freight by ship or railway, in order to reduce the amount of exhaust given off by trucks and automobiles.

45

THE JAPANESE

THE MAJORITY OF THE JAPANESE are a Mongoloid subgroup, that is, they generally have the Mongoloid physical features of yellowish skin, epicanthic eyes, prominent cheekbones, and black hair.

The origin of the race is controversial. There is one theory that Japanese were living on the Japanese islands from the Stone Age. Another suggests that since the early Stone Age there has been an eastward migration on the Asian continent, the farthest point reached being Japan. When Japan was separated from the mainland, the Japanese race developed out of mixed migrants from China, Manchuria, and Korea. Yet another theory suggests that there could have been migrants to the region from the Oceanic or Malay regions.

Opposite: **A mother picking up her children from a day-care center.**

Below: **An Ainu girl of Hokkaido.**

THE AINU

One thing is clear, however: before the migrants—whoever they were—arrived, a race called the Ainu lived in Japan. The Ainu are markedly non-Mongoloid, with the Caucasoid features of fair skin, abundant body hair, rounded eyes, and flatter cheekbones. Recently, the speculation that the Ainu were Caucasoid broke down with the discovery that they lack certain genes present in Caucasians. Studies relate them to the Uralic, Altaic, and Tungusic populations of Russian Siberia. Over the centuries, the Japanese migrants drove the resisting Ainu northward to Hokkaido, where they live today.

The Ainu religion is animistic, one which believes all natural objects, such as animals, trees, and stones, possess a spirit. The bear plays a prominent role in many Ainu folk tales. Many present-day Shinto rites are derived from Ainu rituals and a few Ainu place names, including Mount Fuji, form part of the Japanese vocabulary.

Uniforms are seen everywhere in Japan. High-school uniforms are black or navy blue. These first-year high-school students appear to be a little uncomfortable in their new collars.

THE JAPANESE CHARACTER

The Japanese are a very disciplined people whose society is divided into many compact groups. Being attracted to a group and the desire to be immersed in a group are basic to the Japanese character. The Japanese have to belong to a unit—such as a family—because it gives them a sense of security. To a large extent, they surrender their individuality in exchange for the security of belonging to a group.

The basic unit is the home, as in most human societies. But although they retain the bond of the family or extended family all through life, the Japanese go further and transfer this bond to almost all other spheres of their lives: school, university, and work. In the legal field, Japanese lawyers refer to the groups they belong to as the *mura* ("moo-rah"), meaning village.

Strong attachments to groups have disadvantages. Emotions can be raised to exclude outsiders, even to the extent of forgetting the wider or umbrella group to which one also belongs. Conforming to styles and

A group of senior citizens enjoys a local event together.

rituals can stifle individualism, and the group leader can at times extract blind obedience, exploiting the group for selfish ends. It is also possible to be locked into a small group all one's life.

PROS AND CONS OF THE GROUP SYSTEM The disadvantages of group compactness can be seen in many areas of Japanese life. There is poor cooperation among the three different Buddhist organizations. Research teams made up of experts from different universities do not work together successfully in Japan. The merger of two of the largest breweries was prevented by the blind loyalty of employees to their individual company and their total faith in its management style. There is no "all-Japan" intellectual journal because several attempts to get various intellectual groups to work together have failed.

There are also advantages in group loyalty. The Japanese have learned over the years to extract maximum human effort through the spirit of compact teams. It is one of the most important reasons for their industrial success.

Group leaders generally do not bully their teams or forcibly push their ideas on the group. They have an almost paternal sense of responsibility for their group members and a constant awareness that everyone must play a part in decision-making to ensure that the group stays united.

RELATIONSHIPS

Strong cohesive forces operate within the Japanese group to weld it together. These are the *oya-ko* ("oh-yah-koh") and *sempai-kohai* ("sampie koh-high") relationships built up from early childhood.

Oya-ko means parent-child. It describes the relationship between parents and children in Japan. The respectful attitude of the child toward the parent is fostered, but the responsibility of the parent is equally emphasized.

The *sempai-kohai* relationship is between a senior and a junior, whether at work, in a voluntary organization, or at the university. It is a powerful force that tempers the enthusiasm and hotheadedness of youth and keeps seniors in close touch with the thoughts and feelings of their juniors.

An *oya-ko* relationship is fostered very early between parent and child.

THE HIERARCHICAL SOCIETY The *oya-ko* and *sempai-kohai* relationships put everyone on a series of steps: one is a parent and also a child, a *sempai* or a *kohai* under different circumstances. These relationships arrange Japanese people in a series of layers, making it a hierarchical society. Everyone is ranked. The ranking gives every member of the community a particular place. It is a solution to the conflicts of competition, ambition, and envy; if one's position is fixed and clear, these feelings are defused.

How do the Japanese resolve the "unequalness" that is part of a hierarchical system? Quite simply, the question of inequality does not arise as the ranking is completely accepted in their hearts. Many other societies are split into layers of levels and ranks. With the Japanese it is a deep-seated belief that spills over into other areas. The Japanese have a tendency to rank everything: universities, products, and skills, for example. It comes with the desire to obtain all things *ichiryu* ("i-chi-ri-you"), or first-class, if it can be afforded. In a way, it is a striving for top quality.

SOCIAL MOBILITY The groups and preordained levels are almost exclusive, but there are ways out of the system—opportunities to move in and out of groups and up and down the ladder of ranks exist, though these are difficult. Built into the system are complicated ways to cross barriers, which ensures that only the exceptional individual can climb over these hurdles that the ordinary person is not permitted to surmount.

The Japanese *sempai-kohai* relationship is an important one. Every Japanese speaks of his or her *sempai*, a kind of personal mentor. In a few years, these children will speak of their very own *sempai*.

Two Japanese women in conversation. The attitude of each is respectful and unhurried; to seem impatient would be regarded as an insult.

A SENSE OF DUTY

All Japanese are conscious of their obligations. The obligation to return favors received and to do the right thing for one's group is so complex that several words are required to cover all its meanings—*gimu* ("gi-moo") and *giri* ("gi-ri"), both of which mean "duty," and *on* ("ohn"), which means "favor." To the Japanese, doing one's duty is of the utmost importance.

"SAVING FACE"

Intertwined with the sense of duty and the *sempai-kohai* relationship is the concept of personal image or "face" and the emotions and behavior it inspires. One must treat one's *sempai* with reverence and be gentle with one's *kohai*, always conscious of their feelings..Disgracing oneself affects them, too, and causes them shame, or loss of "face." Appearances and "face" have to be maintained at all times.

This means that the inner self has to be masked most of the time. Thus, Japanese avoid giving a clear answer that commits them fully and shrink from any direct confrontation. It is not deceit or shiftiness. It is necessary to use masks to keep interpersonal relationships smooth. They describe their "split personality" with two words: *tatemae* ("tah-tay-mah-eh") is the facade (what appears in front, the external image) and *honne* ("hohn-nay") is the real root: the true, inner self.

THE REVENGE OF THE 47 RONIN

A story to illustrate the Japanese sense of duty.

Lord Kira, a great *daimyo*, had to instruct Lord Asano in the etiquette for a special ceremony. Unfortunately, the gifts Lord Asano offered to Lord Kira in exchange for the instruction fell short of expectations, so Lord Kira did not teach Lord Asano all he needed to know. On the big day, to his unbounded horror, Lord Asano found that he was not dressed correctly. He drew his sword and attacked Lord Kira, wounding him on the forehead.

In great shame, Lord Asano dressed for *seppuku* ("sep-poo-koo"), or ritual suicide, said farewell to Oishi, his trusted retainer, and killed himself. Since he had no heir, his estate was confiscated and his retainers became *ronin* ("roh-nin")—masterless *samurai*—drifting without a lord to serve. The *ronin,* led by Oishi, had to avenge their master's humiliation. The full burden of unfulfilled obligation hung on them. At a meeting, Oishi selected 47 *ronin*. They made a blood pact and the vendetta began.

All Tokyo was expecting some move, so first Lord Kira had to be thrown off the scent. The 47 *ronin* frequented the worst drinking houses to give the impression that they had lost all pride and honor. Oishi divorced his wife and let his sword rust. One *ronin* killed his father-in-law, another sold his wife as a prostitute to get funds, while the sister of a third was sent to work in Lord Kira's household as a maid.

On the fateful night, Oishi threw a party for Lord Kira's guards at which they all got drunk. The *ronin* raided Lord Kira's stronghold and rushed to his room. He was not there, but his bed was still warm. They spread out and searched. Peeping into an outhouse, they saw a man crouching inside. One *ronin* lunged at him, driving his spear through the wooden wall, but when he withdrew it there was no blood on the blade.

Actually, it was Lord Kira and the spear *had* wounded him, but he had wiped the blood off the sword with his sleeve. The *ronin* burst into the outhouse and recognized him from the scar left on his forehead by Lord Asano's sword. They demanded that he commit *seppuku* at once, but the coward refused. They cut off Lord Kira's head and set out in a procession, with the sword and the head, to Lord Asano's grave. The *ronin* had paid off their obligation.

Karaoke in a Japanese club lounge—one way to release suppressed inner tensions. In addition to musical accompaniment, the video player provides the words of the song, thus prompting the amateur singer.

BODY LANGUAGE

Japanese are extremely observant and send out the most subtle body-language messages. They call this *haragei* ("hah-rah-gay") or the belly feel, listening to the subconscious voice that interprets the minutest sign: a twitch of a facial muscle, an eye movement, or a gesture.

When two Japanese meet, the process begins with the ritual of bowing. The angle of the bow, the delay before straightening up, the number of bows—all add up to outline the positions they are taking in relation to each other, just as attitudes can be read or shown in body language with the jutting-out chin, folded arms, slight dip of the head from the neck, or firm handclasp. In Japanese novels, the reaction of the eyes is described much more often than in Western writing.

APPARENT INDISCIPLINE The Japanese are a highly disciplined people, yet sometimes their behavior appears shockingly wild and uncontrolled. They get quite drunk in public, at festivals they seem unrestrained in their enjoyment, and they publicly enjoy various forms of pornography.

This behavior stems from the Japanese philosophy of life. To the Japanese, suppression of a tendency to pleasure is unnatural. Yet, every pleasure must be relegated to its proper place, as a temporary distraction from the serious business of life. Seeing from that perspective, the Japanese feel their soul is not corrupted by occasional excesses.

WOMEN IN JAPAN

Women have not yet broken away from tradition and achieved equality in Japan. For many years, the authorities have tried to elevate women's status, but there exists an odd mixture of progress and traditionalism with regard to women in Japanese society.

Throughout the centuries, Japanese women have pushed themselves forward to challenge and match male dominance. There are few countries in the world in which women have played such a major role in the arts as in Japan, including Murasaki Shikibu, author of the *Tale of Genji* in A.D. 1000, a novel studied around the world today (see page 97). Chinese records of Japanese history describe a queen, Himiko, who brought an end to the wars between the small states and established a unified nation. Her state was called Yamatai, and when she died, 100 slaves were buried with her.

Two young girls, one in modern dress, the other in a simple traditional dress, a *kimono* ("kee-moh-noh").

The woman in Japan is relegated to a subservient role. It would be unusual for a Japanese man to open the door for a Japanese woman or let her go through the door first. Even though many women work, a Japanese woman's place is supposed to be in the home, and there she has some power. The Japanese husband gives his wife his entire salary and she budgets for the household, giving him an allowance.

There have been exceptional women in the last two decades who have run large companies, written bestsellers, and led the field in fashion design. The average Japanese woman, however, no matter how steeped in Western lifestyle when single, reverts to a traditional role when she marries.

LIFESTYLE

THE DISCIPLINED LIFESTYLE of the Japanese evolved out of their physical environment. The harsh climate of cold winters and heavy snowfalls in the north, hot summers, typhoons, and, above all the earthquakes and volcanoes, have made them rugged and ready to adapt their living conditions to changing forces.

The Japanese once lived in small houses that could be rebuilt easily after earthquakes and fires. They depended greatly on protein from the sea, but slow transportation to the interior of the islands made it necessary for them resort to eating seafood that was preserved with salt and vinegar and placed on top of rice seasoned with vinegar. In the north, they learned to pickle vegetables to last them through the long winters. As the population grew, overcrowding became a major problem.

In essence, Japanese lifestyle has not changed for centuries. Although most Japanese people today don Western fashion, it is not uncommon for Japanese men and women to dress in traditional fashion to attend weddings or other formal gatherings.

If for only short respites, the Japanese enjoy the pleasures they have immensely. They add a glint of beauty to the everyday and the mundane. A good example of this is the Japanese way of packaging. There are rules and forms of how to wrap and embellish a present. As important as the choice of the offering is the visual pleasure given when presenting the gift—the symbolic communication of the paper or silk wrapper, its folding, color, pattern, and the added decoration that gives the subtle touch of completeness.

Another example of the Japanese love of aesthetics is the way food is arranged and served. The visual experience adds to the enjoyment of a meal and great care is taken in its presentation.

Opposite: **A man praying in a temple. Religion is very much a part of the Japanese lifestyle.**

Below: **A quirky way of presenting shrimp.**

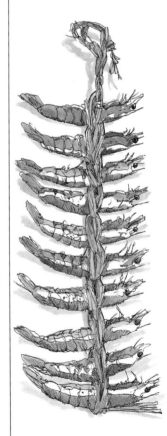

HOMES

Housing is a great problem in the cities, where 80 percent of Japan's population (127 million) live. Yokohama and Tokyo, the largest cities, together house about 27 million. Houses are small, but as they have always been small, the Japanese accept the minimal space standards. With urban sprawl and limited high-rise housing development (because of earthquakes), many are forced to live one to two hours, by train, from the city centers.

The traditional Japanese house has no tables or chairs. The Japanese sit on straw mats called *tatami* ("tah-tah-mee"), and it is usual to measure house and room in terms of the *tatami*, each about 3 feet by 6 feet (0.9

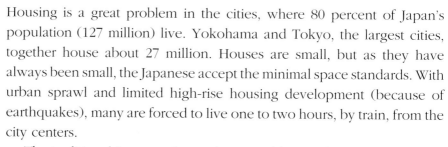

m by 1.8 m). Bedding consists of light mattresses and blankets that are put away into cabinets every morning so as not to clutter the small rooms. Since Japanese often sit on the floor, they remove their shoes as soon as they enter the house and put on house slippers. They change their house slippers for bathroom slippers before entering the bathroom. Today, tables and chairs are often used and many houses are built with Western and Japanese sections.

The focal point in a Japanese living room is an alcove called the *tokonoma* ("toh-koh-noh-mah") where a scroll, painting, or flower arrangement is placed. In the old days, little stoves covered with blankets warmed feet and legs. These warmers are still used in the country, but in the cities portable electric heaters are the norm at home, and commercial buildings are centrally heated. A typical Japanese home in the city has all the electrical conveniences that one takes for granted in a Western home.

In the country, where space is not a problem, construction standards

Top: **Slippers, called** ***surippa*** **("soo-rip-pah"), came to Japan from the West. Note the two sets, outdoor and home wear.**

Bottom: **Typical bedroom with a mattress that can be rolled neatly out of the way in daytime.**

An aerial view of congested Tokyo.

and environmental conditions of houses are well below those of houses in the cities. A nation that has led the world in mass-producing articles to allow one to get more out of life at any income level has left its country folk living with the technology of the 1950s and 1960s.

Above: **Geisha** ("gay-shah") means artist and *geishas* are artists of social graces. A *geisha* studies dancing and singing, makeup and dress, flower arrangement, and the ritual tea ceremony. She can be recognized by her distinctive *kimono, obi,* platform sandals, and exotically made-up face.

Above right: The *kimono* is preferred for ceremonial occasions, especially by Japanese women. Young Japanese women wear the *furisode* (foo-ree-soh-deh), a bright *kimono* with flowing sleeves worn by young, single women, to a New Year's Day celebration at a Shinto shrine.

DRESS

The Japanese dress with care and forethought. In fact, Japanese fashion design is now recognized as belonging to the realm of high fashion. Several designers have won international fashion awards. One of them, Hanae Mori (nicknamed "Iron Butterfly" because of the butterfly motif identifying her collections), has received France's most coveted cultural award, the Croix de Chevalier des Arts et des Lettres. Japanese dress has come a long way from the *kimono*.

The traditional *kimono,* a one-piece wraparound garment held in place by an *obi* ("oh-bee"), or sash, is still preferred for ceremonial occasions. Today, one hardly sees the *kimono,* although the light evening *yukata* ("yoo-kah-tah"), which is like a *kimono,* is worn at home.

Western-style dress has replaced traditional wear to such an extent that in another generation the Japanese will need lessons on how to wear a *kimono.* Businessmen wear dark suits with white shirts. They use their version of English words for these: *sebiro* ("seh-bee-roh"), meaning from Savile Row for the suit, and *waishatsu* ("wy-shah-tsoo"), or white shirt.

Men and women who work in factories all wear uniforms. The general rule is that unless the employee has to meet with a customer, he or she wears a company uniform.

GOOD MANNERS

The Japanese have rules for almost every human activity and even today many of the old rules of correct behavior are faithfully observed. Take bowing for example—it has a whole series of set forms: the very deep, respectful bow, bowing when seated, how to position the hands while bowing, the need to come to a stop before bowing rather than bowing in mid-stride.

Visiting etiquette is similar to that in English Victorian society: whom and when to visit, the proper entrance, refolding the towel offered to the visitor before putting it down, how to drink tea and eat cakes, polite leave-taking, and other niceties.

There are also rules for gifts: the times of year when gifts are expected, when fans should be given, when pickles should be given, and above all, the way the gift is wrapped, for, no matter how thoughtful the gift, one could still insult the recipient by not folding the paper correctly.

There is also proper etiquette for weddings and funerals. One should never say *sayonara* ("sah-yoh-nah-rah"), or goodbye, to the bride and groom, for example, because the word is too final. One should also never call on someone on the way home from attending a funeral.

Underlying all the forms of etiquette is the principle that nothing should be communicated directly. Symbols, hints, and getting to the point in roundabout fashion are the characteristics of social interaction in Japan. Saying the wrong thing directly could embarrass the other party, even if it is praise or flattery, because both demand the correct response; otherwise, there is loss of face.

Above : **Bowing at the right angle.**

Below: **A *furoshiki*, or cloth wrapper.**

Shibuya is Tokyo's satellite town for younger people. Well-provided with burger joints and youthful entertainment, it is frequented by students.

RELAXATION

Although Japanese life is strictly channeled into the grooves engraved by social norms, the Japanese have opportunities to break away from the restrictions of their patterned living.

Besides condoning drunkenness, Japanese society also provides social escape through festivals. The Japanese let themselves go at festivals. They let the rhythm of the drums get to them; they sing and dance, pushing themselves physically and mixing freely into the small hours of the morning.

People in Paris, London, Frankfurt, or Los Angeles who meet visiting Japanese businessmen regularly, who have eaten and drunk with them, shown them the city lights, and had pleasant and memorable evenings with them, often do not realize that behind the same polite, smiling, impassive faces are people who, on occasion, can really let loose.

A gloomy, cold January day for these courting couples leaving a Shinto shrine.

COURTSHIP

The influence of Western lifestyle is evident in all Japanese cities, but subtle differences exist that are not at first obvious. Such is the case with social contact between young boys and girls, or between men and women.

Arranged introductions with a view to marriage still occur, but today, after the meeting, the young people are left to work it out themselves. Romantic love in the Western sense is strong and will determine the match or mismatch decision. After this, an ingrained sense of duty will be the rock on which a marriage will develop and grow.

This does not mean that the Japanese are not romantic. There is a mixture of a traditional sense of duty and the romantic love of a married couple that their poets sing about. This is a somewhat restrained yielding to personal feelings, which is one of many escapes the Japanese lifestyle allows in the face of the society's rigid discipline.

THE FAMILY

The Japanese man gives his life to the company he works for; it is his focus, his real world. The woman gives hers to her home and family. Despite the influence of Western ideas, these basics have not changed, although a slow shift from tradition can be seen in the younger Japanese today.

PARENTS The businessman father spends hardly any time with his family during the week. He leaves early and returns late, not necessarily because he is wining and dining until the wee hours of the morning (although he may have to entertain clients), but because he has a long distance to travel. In addition, an executive who arrives home early loses status in the eyes of the neighbors, who will conclude that he is not important enough to entertain clients. This is changing, however; there is a move toward shorter work hours and more emphasis on the family.

The mother controls family expenditure, and thereby exerts her indirect influence on the household, but her role is inferior to the man of the house. Nevertheless, the status quo is slowly changing as more and more professional women are battling the odds and making their presence felt in commercial and public life.

CHILDREN Children spend their early years struggling with language. Before they begin school, they must learn different verbal languages for addressing superiors, equals, and inferiors, in addition to important body

Junior-high examinations are highly competitive and parents send their children to *juku* ("joo-koo"), or cram schools, where they receive special tutoring. Fees are high and the pressure is intense.

languages. In school, they must master approximately 100 phonetic characters and 1,945 of the much more complex Chinese characters that the government has classified as the most commonly used *kanji* ("kahn-jee"), or characters.

Appreciation of the arts is emphasized and instilled in students early. They study the aesthetics and beauty of brush strokes in calligraphy and painting. They are taken to scenic and historic places and are taught *origami* ("aw-ree-gah-mee"), which is the creation of forms through paper-folding. They also either sing or learn to play a musical instrument.

For many children the goal is to pass the examinations that will get them into a prestigious university—a difficult ordeal, for the workload is heavy, memories are stretched, and perseverance is severely tested. If they succeed, however, they are set for life, as their future lifestyle will depend on which university they attend. The Japanese classify people by which university they attended, a tendency adopted from the Western world but held to with much greater rigidity in Japan.

Parents may enroll their children in expensive *juku* ("joo-koo"), private cram schools that give intensive tutoring to help students qualify for a good school; this in turn will help them qualify for a more reputable university.

Movie posters draw passersby to the movie theater.

ADOLESCENCE TO ADULTHOOD In the cities, teenagers and young adults under the age of 30 enjoy life. They have sufficient money (whether earned or as an allowance) to spend on clothes, CDs and tapes, motorcycles, Walkmans, Discmans, and the other material objects that help to generate the modern, Western-influenced concept of fun.

Japanese teenagers enjoy American music, television, movies, and writing. Their parents felt the same in their teens, but as they grew older they were more influenced by traditional Japanese culture. All the signs indicate that this generation will become more traditional as it ages, too.

The lifestyles of the young and the middle-aged are as different in Japan as they are all over the world. However, the discipline of their upbringing and the cultural chasm between Japanese and Westerners still exist, holding Japan back from irreversible "internationalism."

Teens gather near Meiji Shrine, in the Harajuku area of Tokyo, where they like to display the most outrageous fashion.

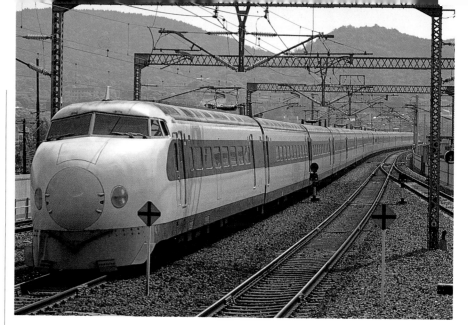

A "bullet" train can reach a maximum speed of 186 miles (300 km) per hour.

A TYPICAL DAY

The working day of a typical Japanese man begins very early. He lives many miles from the city where he works, and probably takes buses and the suburban train to get to work, a journey of about 90 minutes on average. He makes sure to arrive early.

If he works in a factory, the work day starts with an assembly. He and his colleagues do some limbering-up exercises, sing the company song, and may get a pep-talk from the manager before they report to their jobs.

He works with great concentration all day, putting heart and soul into every little operation, as is ingrained in him. He must not fail. He must not let his company down. Although he is only a factory worker, he sees the president quite often because the president walks through the factory regularly. He knows that if something disturbs him badly he can approach the president. Yet, he will never do this without much deliberation and discussion with his colleagues, because such an approach will have to be on behalf of the group.

When the day ends, he will drop into a small bar for a beer or *sake* ("sah-kay"), Japanese rice wine, with his co-workers. If he is a company executive, he will have an expense account to use, not only for his customers but also for his staff. The company realizes that drinking together helps bring the team closer.

He will probably go to an *akachochin* ("ah-kah-choh-chin"), a Japanese-style pub, where he may enjoy *karaoke* ("kah-rah-oh-kay") singing.

Young families gather at a park in downtown Tokyo during the summer holidays.

Everyone will have to take a turn, whether it is singing to recorded accompaniment or reciting a poem. They will have great fun, but must be careful not to upset anyone.

When the Japanese working man returns home, his wife gives him all her attention. This is changing, but very slowly. The ideal wife in the minds of Japanese men and women is the woman completely devoted to her family, who responds to every whim of her husband and very often of her children—her sons in particular.

During the weekend, he takes his family out, unless he is one of the very few who can afford to play golf. (If he has that privilege, he will spend all the time he can on the golf course and play with intense enthusiasm.) Tennis, skiing, or a short day trip to some historic or scenic place will be on top of the family list of preferences. There may be hundreds of people there, but they will not mind. If there is a festival that weekend, they will participate in it.

RELIGION

RELIGION IS an integral part of Japanese life. Although it is ever-present it does not interfere with everyday life. If asked whether she or he is religious a Japanese will reply "no," yet will be seen to observe all the Shinto rites and visit Buddhist temples without being conscious of participating in anything special. In a country of about 126 million people there are approximately 188,000 buildings of worship—an average of approximately 660 persons per place of worship.

The primary religions are Shinto and Buddhism. It has been said that Shinto takes care of daily living, while Buddhism takes care of the afterlife. Most Japanese follow both religions without being concerned about which is right or true. It is an attitude that Westerners find hard to understand. When J. Seward wrote, "The Japanese have tended to mold their religions to fit their way of life more than the reverse," he highlighted one aspect of the Japanese attitude toward religion.

SHINTO

Shinto, literally "the way of the gods," does not have a clear principle or a definite family of deities. Rather, it encompasses a belief held by the Japanese from earlier times that there is a certain spiritual essence in all things, living or nonliving, even in rocks, the wind, the sea, and echoes sounded off in a forest of tall trees or a mountain range. They call this *kami* ("kah-mee"). The Japanese character for *kami* signifies above or superior. *Kami* is often translated as God, but it does not really embody the Western concept of God; rather, it is more a sense of superior forces that are at work in the world.

Opposite: **A typical scene during New Year's Day in Japan, when millions of Japanese flock to temples and shrines around the country to seek blessings for the year ahead.**

Above: **The Grand Shrine of Ise is the most important Shinto shrine. Its form has been preserved for over a thousand years. Every 20 years it is "renewed"—torn down and rebuilt.**

Right: A Shinto ceremony.

Opposite: **A tree of paper blessings. These are strips of paper picked by the worshiper through one of many means: it could be with the help of a bird or the result of shaking a bamboo container of "fortune sticks." If the piece of paper contains an inauspicious message, the worshiper may tie it to a tree or gate, or some other structure in the temple grounds. The tree shown in this photo is used for messages related to finding a good partner in marriage.**

SHRINES To the Japanese, the emperor is a *kami,* but he is not God. Spirits of national heroes, famous scholars and officials, rivers, mountains, trees, and cliffs are *kami*. The Japanese build shrines to show their gratitude for protection, and they pray at these shrines for success.

The taboos are primitive and do not affect Japanese lives substantially. There are no rules of self-discipline. The Shinto belief is that man is born good and should therefore follow his natural impulses.

RITES AND SYMBOLS Shinto does not have the paraphernalia of most religions. Sticks, leaves, and strips of paper are used for generally simple rituals. One essential feature of Shinto rites are the symbolic purification acts a Japanese performs before approaching a Shinto shrine—the washing of hands and mouth, for example. Shinto rituals are part of Japanese birth and wedding ceremonies as well as part of ceremonies for launching ships and laying foundation stones for new buildings.

SHINTO IN JAPANESE HISTORY Shinto has been subject to manipulation in the past. Although the Shinto priests cleared up some of the vagueness of their religion when Buddhism entered the country, it could not compete with the elaborate Buddhist rituals, the well-defined Buddhist moral code, its philosophical approach, and to some extent, the architectural arts and special foods.

In 1700 there was a revival of Shinto, and after the Meiji Restoration, the government used Shinto as a unifying force. Financing was provided, and Shinto became almost, though not quite, a state religion. In the late 1800s the government thought it necessary to separate Shinto into two 'sects.' The first sect dealt with all matters concerning the imperial family, while the second sect dealt with religious rituals, such as births and weddings.

In December 1945 the American occupation authorities persuaded the Japanese government to stop financing Shinto, breaking the link between the religion and the state. Shinto temples moved into business ventures, selling off part of their land or using it and their funds to invest in temple parking lots, kindergartens, wedding halls, and agricultural enterprises.

Shinto survived and today there are about 80,000 Shinto priests serving in about 90,000 shrines.

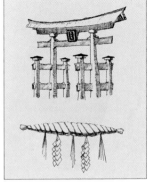

The *torii*, a graceful gateway, is the symbol of a Shinto shrine. The *shimenawa* (shee-may-nah-wah") is a straw festoon fixed around trees in the shrine compound to mark sacred ground.

BUDDHISM

Buddhism came to Japan in A.D. 552. This religion brought to the people of Japan a philosophy of life that was both simple and intellectually satisfying. Buddhism appealed to the Japanese because it was clear in its principles and in its taboos and yet impressive in its rituals, art, and architecture. Buddhism swept across Japan, filling a vacuum left by Shinto.

Buddhism penetrated Japanese society at its highest levels. Prince Regent Shotoku (574–622) persuaded his aunt, the Empress Suiko, that Buddhism did not conflict with Shinto. Buddhism then became a state religion.

Even though popular with the nobility, Buddhism only became popular with the masses from about the 13th century. It influenced both the philosophy and food of Japan, but it never managed to replace Shinto. Probably the most important influence Buddhism had in Japan is on the way the Japanese regard death—as an accepted part of the divine scheme of all things. Buddha's dying words, "All things are transitory," have made a deep impression on the character of the Japanese.

Jizo Buddha, the popular god of children, dressed as an offering to the gods. Such a doll is bought, adorned, and offered with a wish—this one is probably for a baby.

ZEN AND OTHER BUDDHIST SECTS

When the Japanese absorb a foreign concept, they add to it or give it a Japanese character. Two monks, Eisai (1141–1215) and Dogen (1200–1253), brought Zen Buddhism from China to Japan. Zen Buddhism appealed to the Japanese. The essence of Zen is: "Look within yourself; you yourself are the Buddha." It is a philosophy of meditation and its fundamental belief is that in every human being there is something precious and divine.

In 1253 another Buddhist sect was founded by a man from the Kanto region—Nichiren (1222–1282).

He was a colorful and outstanding monk who placed his whole faith in the *Lotus Sutra* book of Buddhism. He appealed to the common person by linking Buddhism with natural life. His predictions of future events won him fame, particularly when he foretold the Mongol invasion of Japan. He took a clear stand by attacking other religions.

A monk begs for monetary donations. Some sects beg for food.

The Soka Gakkai is a lay religious group based on the teachings of Nichiren. The organization was established in 1946; today it has more than 6 million adherents in Japan. In the 1950s the Soka Gakkai spread its teachings with almost military zeal with a campaign of *shakabuku* ("shah-kah-boo-koo")—literally "to shatter and subdue"—and used psychology to convert the unconvinced. It started a political party, the Komeito (Clean Government Party), but it does not play a major role in the party today.

CHRISTIANITY

About 1 percent of the Japanese are Christians. Like many minority groups, they have developed an instinct for survival. The Japanese Christians, like the Christians of Roman times, have a history of faith and perseverance that is quite remarkable.

Francis Xavier and other Christian missionaries came to Japan in 1594. By 1635 they had made between 200,000 and 300,000 converts. There were factors that worked in their favor and the counting of true Christians is questionable, but the fact is that a large and powerful Christian community was established.

Christianity reached the highest levels of the *shogun* administration, but interdenominational rivalry weakened the foundations the pioneers had laid: Christians were eventually persecuted. The struggle reached a climax in the siege and massacre of 37,000 at Shimabara in 1638. To this day, historians argue about the religious and political aspects of the Christian resistance. By 1650 Christianity had been mostly eliminated.

Japan isolated itself from the world after 1638, but when missionaries were allowed in after Commodore Perry opened Japan's doors in 1857, a church was built in Nagasaki and 4,000 Japanese Christians came to the church to rejoice. They had kept their faith alive and secret for 225 years.

RELIGIOUS ORGANIZATIONS IN JAPAN

These figures are of the number of religious organizations in Japan and their membership in 1997. They show the similar numbers of Shinto and Buddhist members. Another peculiar feature is that the total number of members exceeds the population of Japan (194 million in 1996)—this is because many Japanese are registered both as Shinto and as Buddhist.

Religion is not taught in schools, and marriage between members of different religions is not a problem. In fact, it is not unusual for newlyweds to report their wedding to their ancestors at the family altar, have a Christian wedding ceremony, then honeymoon around Shinto shrines and Buddhist temples.

"Japanese culture has no conception of a God existing abstractly, completely separated from the human world."

- Nakane Chie

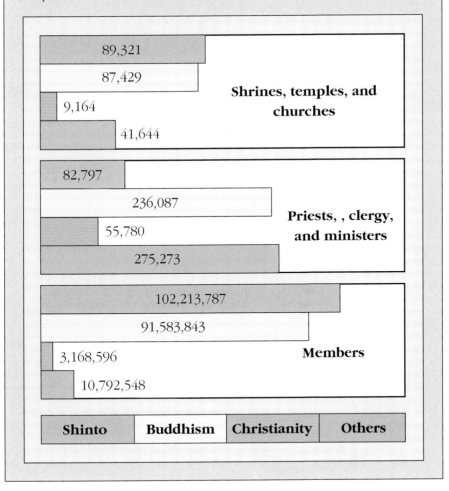

| | Shinto | Buddhism | Christianity | Others |

Shrines, temples, and churches
89,321
87,429
9,164
41,644

Priests, , clergy, and ministers
82,797
236,087
55,780
275,273

Members
102,213,787
91,583,843
3,168,596
10,792,548

LANGUAGE

JAPANESE IS a well-developed language similar to European languages in grammar and to Chinese in script. Unlike spoken Chinese, formal Japanese tends to be monotonal, although one syllable in every word is always stressed more than the others. Nouns are not varied; there is no difference between the plural and the singular. As is the case in English, Japanese places the adjective before the noun it qualifies.

However, Japanese people do not always include the subject of a sentence when speaking, as the subject is usually implied by the context of the conversation. Ambiguities such as this one make Japanese a challenging language for a foreigner to master.

SOCIAL TONES

The need to be continuously aware of one's position is carried to the extreme. The pronouns *you* and *I* have many variants to reflect deference for age and status. Words are selected to reflect the status difference between speaker and listener at all times.

Different verbs, verb endings, and ways of using the same words must be considered. The verb *to come*, for example, ranges from the crude *koi* ("coy"), shouted to children and army privates, to the soft *irasshaimase* ("ee-ras-shah-ee-mah-say"), meaning *please come in,* that one hears on entering a Japanese restaurant. The verb *to be* has a similar range. The most polite form is *de gozaimasu* ("day goh-zah-i-mah-sue"), which is generally used in public announcements. Women always use the polite form. Girls eventually have to learn to change from rough and simple children's language to the softer, polite adult female form.

INDIRECTNESS In speech, the Japanese prefer to be indirect. American-style straight-from-the-shoulder frankness is considered rude. Conversational sentences are thus longer than in English. This indirectness often appears in the written form.

Opposite: **A young lady practices the traditional art of calligraphy, a mandatory subject in Japanese schools.**

VERBS

Verbs are often joined to make new verbs. *Tachiyomi* is such a verb: *tachi* ("tah-chee"), meaning to stand, and *yomi* ("yoh-mee"), meaning to read. It means stand and read. The word filled a need to describe a common pastime and a common sight in bookshops.

PRONUNCIATION

Japanese pronunciation is straightforward and clear. It is not a tonal language. There may be two or three meanings for the same sound, but the context in most cases makes the meaning clear. There are no words ending in consonants (except *ng*), and no diphthongs.

There are regional variations in phrasing, accents, and terms and idioms used, as there is in English across the United States, but there are no dialects as there are in China.

SOUNDS OF WORDS		PRONUNCIATION
There are a great many examples of onomatopoeia (words with sounds that reflect their meaning) in Japanese.		*a* as in art
		ai as in aisle
		e as in get
ha-ha	**gasp, pant**	*ei* as in veil
ki-ki	**squeaky**	*g* (always hard) as in
goro-goro	**rumbling**	go
pota-pota	**water dripping**	*i* as in tin
kusu-kusu	**giggle**	*n* as in sing
bechakucha	**chatterbox**	*o* as in pole
		u as in rude

Japanese is not an easy language to learn. Take, for example, the verb *to bring*, which has two forms: *motte-kuru* ("mot-tay koo-roo") for things and *tsurete-kuru* ("tsoo-ray-tay koo-roo) for people. But it is not quite as simple as that. One uses *tsurete-kuru* if one brings a dog, but *motte-kuru* if bringing a goldfish or bird. The difference is not because the latter are carried, since bringing an infant still requires *tsurete-kuru*.

"ADOPTED" ENGLISH

Many English words adopted by the Japanese have been distorted from the original. A prewar women's fashion word, *two-piece*, for example, was adapted into *one-piece* ("won-pee-sue"), which describes a dress. The word *glass* has two forms to reduce its ambiguity: *garasu* ("gah-rah-sue") for plate glass and *gurasu* ("goo-rah-sue") for drinking glass.

Often the original word is unrecognizable. *Juice* becomes *juusu* ("jee-yoo-soo"), and because they do not differentiate between l and r, *lemon* becomes *remon*. English words are shortened: *biru* ("bee-roo") means building; *sutando* ("soo-tahn-doh") means standard lamp. Other examples are *boonasu* ("boh-nah-soo"), bonus; *chii-zu* ("chee-zoo"), cheese; *gorufu* ("gaw-roo-foo"), golf; and *maikaa* ("my-kah"), my car.

JAPANESE EXAMPLES

NAMES Most Japanese girls' names end with *ko,* which means little or child. Typical names are Yukiko (*yuki* means snow), Hanako (*hana* means flower), and Sachiko (*sachi* means happiness).

The surname is placed first, but almost without exception, Japanese businessmen overseas reverse this order. Thus TAKAHASHI Kintaro becomes Kintaro TAKAHASHI on his overseas business card.

Mr. This is *san* ("sahn"). *San* is also Mrs. and Miss. A respectful version of Mr. is *sama* ("sah-mah"). It is hardly ever used today for individuals. It is used for addressing groups much in the same way that one says "ladies and gentlemen" in English, or when referring to a god: *kamisama* ("kah-mi-sah-mah").

"BELLY" The Japanese place the seat of emotions in the stomach, as some English expressions, like *gut-feeling,* do. In Japanese one says "the stomach is hungry." "Not showing one's stomach" means concealing one's real intentions; to "probe the stomach" is to sound out someone's thoughts; to "cut the stomach and speak" is to be open and frank.

Harakiri ("hah-rah-ki-ri") is ritual suicide by cutting the stomach open. The implication is the baring and bleeding of one's soul. In fact, those committing *harakiri* seldom die from the disembowelling cut. Death usually comes from a sword blow to the neck delivered by the ritual attendant.

GESTURES To indicate oneself, Japanese point to the nose, not the heart. When counting on their fingers, they start with the open hand and bring each finger down to the palm in turn.

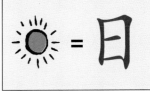

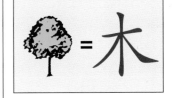

Traditional tools used in the Japanese art of calligraphy include Japanese paper, brushes, and ink set.

SCRIPTS

The Japanese adapted Chinese for their written language. It is generally believed that Chinese characters first came to Japan through Korea, although some writing found in burial mounds suggests that written Chinese may have come directly from China. Chinese characters are simplified drawings called ideograms. An example is given on the right.

KANA The Japanese simplified Chinese characters and devised two phonetic scripts of their own. The sounds are the same for both. These are the *hiragana* (hee-rah-gah-nah") and the *katakana* ("kah-tah-kah-nah"), collectively known as *kana*. The Chinese characters they use are known as *kanji*. The Japanese script uses *kana* interspersed with *kanji,* which may have one or more syllables. *Kanji* is complex and has contributed to Japan's education problems. The Japanese have been trying to reduce the number of *kanji* for many years. In 1946 the education ministry reduced the number of characters to 1,850 and then revised the number again to 1,945, but one has to know many more than these to read Japanese books today. Novelists do not limit their repertoire to 1,945 characters.

The removal of thousands of *kanji* from the official list gave rise to problems with surnames. It was as though the U.S. government decided that "Smith" was an obsolete word and deleted it from all official lists!

ARTS

JAPAN IS ONE of the very few countries in the world where the arts are appreciated by both the intellectuals and the average citizen. Appreciation of the arts is instilled in Japanese children from the earliest years at home. In high school, the arts are represented by twelve separate subjects: three levels each of music, fine arts, crafts, and calligraphy.

VISUAL ARTS

All Japanese derive great pleasure from the visual arts. This includes landscape gardening; *ikebana* ("ee-kay-bah-nah"), the art of flower arrangement; *bonsai* ("bon-zye"), the growing of miniature trees; goldfish breeding; painting; pottery; stone carving; the dyeing of silk; textile printing; making swords, paper, lacquerware, kites, drums, musical instruments, dolls, and masks; paperfolding; and the design of wooden buildings. In Japan, the men and women highly skilled in the arts are called "living national treasures."

Left: The growing of miniature trees through careful pruning is an art called *bonsai*.

Opposite: Swordmaking is an ancient art practiced by only a few Japanese individuals today. Some of these artisans have been honored with the title of Living National Treasure by the Japanese government.

Above and opposite: **Wet and dry Japanese garden landscapes. Like** *bonsai* **Japanese landscaping has its roots in Taoism, an ancient Chinese philosophy that teaches that one's vitality can reach a peak if one is surrounded by landscapes that are replicas of famous sites. In Japan, art forms have departed from this concept and have taken on their own artistic dimensions.**

IKEBANA AND LANDSCAPE GARDENING

The emphasis in both *ikebana* and landscape gardening is on naturalism. Both the flower arranger and garden landscape designer take their inspiration from nature. In *ikebana,* the Japanese art of flower arrangement, the flowing line is the most important consideration, more important than color or form. It may be a fallen branch picked from the roadside or simply a piece of driftwood discovered along the coast, but if it has a beautiful shape or line, it can be used as the basis of an *ikebana* arrangement. Groups of flowers, no matter how striking in color or form, take second place.

Another interesting feature of *ikebana* is that the materials used in the arrangements reflect the passage of time: the past is represented by flowers in full bloom, pods, or dried leaves; the present is represented in half-open blossoms or perfect leaves, and the future in buds.

As in many other Japanese visual arts, the four seasons play a major role in *ikebana,* and arrangements are tailored to the season: in the fall one would see sparse arrangements, and in the summer one would see full, spreading ones.

Landscape gardening is represented by two basic forms: hilly and flat. The presence of water is a vital part of both. Water is represented by sandy waves in a dry landscape (made with sand, stones, rocks, and perhaps the occasional piece of driftwood) and by a pool or stream in evergreen

landscapes. The colors are stark and severe in dry landscapes—light sand and black or gray rocks and stones.

Natural landscapes, on the other hand, may feature a pavilion, and stone lanterns and pagodas. Rocks and stones are subtly placed to represent islands and hills. Also present are evergreens, *bonsai* (usually non-flowering), bridges, and paths.

A painting of a *kabuki* ("kah-boo-key") actor Otani Oniji by the artist Sharaku (see page 89).

PAINTING

Every house has a *kakemono* ("kah-kay-moh-noh"), meaning hanging thing, in the main room. Only one picture is hung, and this is changed every season. One is thus reminded by the picture of the passage of time and the rhythms of life.

Painting in Japan really started in the seventh century A.D., when a Korean monk, Doncho, introduced paper, the techniques of mixing colors, and other innovations. Paintings were done on silk or paper without models or attention to true perspective. A short description of, or a reference to, the painting in the form of a poem was part of the picture; the calligraphy with which this was written was a work of art in itself.

Buddhism had a strong influence on painting from the eighth century to the 14th century. In the Heian period, large horizontal scroll paintings of the life of Buddha were produced. By the Kamakura (1185–1333) period, painting had gone beyond landscapes, trees, and flowers; animals, pictures of everyday life and some caricatures were being painted.

WOODCUTS

In the 18th century, woodblock printing became popular. Woodblock printing combined two skills: the artist's and the woodblock craftsman's. The skill of the woodblock craftsman allowed the reproduction of works of art at an affordable price.

One of the best known artists of that century was Utamaro (1753–1806). *A Book of Insects* was his first volume of prints. He also produced drawings of courtesans and lovers. Sharaku, another artist, was noted for his pictures of popular *noh* ("noh") and *kabuki* actors.

Hokusai (1760–1849) and Hiroshige (1797–1858) were two very prominent woodcut artists in Japan. Hokusai's best-known works are "*Thirty-six Views of Mount Fuji,*" "*One Hundred Views of Mount Fuji,*" "*Scenes of Edo* (Tokyo) *and the Sumida River,*" and "*Famous Bridges and Waterfalls.*"

Hiroshige is known for his "Fifty-three Stages of the Tokaido." The Tokaido was the road between Edo, the seat of the Shogun, and Kyoto, where the emperor reigned with his court. The Tokaido series included not only scenes along the road but also a great wealth of detail about buildings and people of all classes, often with a bit of humor.

POTTERY

Painting was not the only art that flourished in early Japan. From the early Jomon period (10,000–300 B.C.), pottery with surface patterns produced by pressing rope onto wet clay was being made. The potter's wheel came to Japan from Korea with Korean kiln technology in the first three centuries A.D. The Koreans also brought knowledge of bronze-making to Japan. Among early Japanese bronzes were swords and bells that had no practical use. They were objects for magic and rituals, and for burying the dead.

A clay pot with patterns produced by rope. This is a *haniwa* from about A.D. 500.

ARCHITECTURE

Japanese architecture is an architecture of wood, a result of the abundance of mountain timber and the need to have light structures to withstand earthquakes. The basic forms came from China, but the Japanese developed their own styles.

Traditional houses were wood-framed structures where no attempt was made to hide the structural elements. Paper and rushes were used to fill spaces between panels. The paper and wood-frame sliding door was developed; it did not need the space a swinging door required. The wood absorbed some of the summer moisture and released moisture into the air during the dry winter. Thatched roofs, 3 feet (1 m) deep, were popular.

These materials, however, are all combustible, so repositories for valuables, with mud-packed walls, had to be built. Some of Japan's finest structures have burned down, and many of the "old" temples are in fact reconstructions of buildings that were razed by fire.

TEMPLES The oldest structure in Japan is a temple in Nara called Horyuji, the Temple of Noble Law. Construction begun in A.D. 601 and was completed in A.D. 607. It was rebuilt in 712 after a fire. The Horyuji was the center of arts and scholarship, and its teaching influenced intellectuals throughout Japan. It was founded by Prince Shotoku, who defused the conflict between Shinto and Buddhism; it was from Horyuji that Buddhism spread across Japan. Today, the temple houses a huge treasure of priceless objects, including a camphorwood carving of the Buddhist deity Kudara Kannon and the oldest existing embroidery in Japan, called "tapestry of heaven."

The largest wooden structure in the world, also at Nara, is the Great Buddha Hall of the Todaiji or Great Eastern Temple. The present

The Horyuji of Nara, re-built in A.D. 712, is the old-est structure in Japan. The Buddhist images it enshrines are believed to be the originals.

building—161 feet (49 m) high, 187 feet (57 m) long, and 164 feet (50 m) wide—was reconstructed in 1708 after the original burned down. It houses the largest bronze statue in the world, a figure of the Great Sun Buddha, which is 71.5 feet (21.7 m) high.

Japanese temples are usually groups of several structures: a pagoda, a large hall, occasionally a lecture hall, and modest quarters for monks and nuns. The pagodas are beautiful structures built to withstand earthquakes. In the Kanto earthquake of 1923, which destroyed 580,000 houses, the 106-foot (32-m), five-storied pagoda at Kaneiji in Ueno Park, Tokyo, survived.

 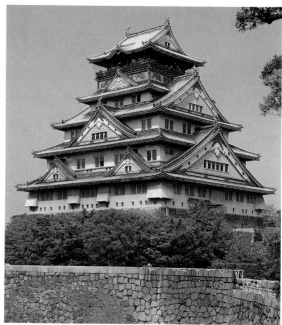

Himeji Castle (left) and Osaka Castle (right).

CASTLES Many Japanese cities were built as castle towns. Castles were built following universal military considerations: a commanding site on high ground or a site protected by water, and maze-like corridors from the entrance to slow down an attacking enemy.

Japanese castles have other special features. They were not built to withstand cannon attack as cannons were rarely used in feudal wars. Only the outer walls were designed for defense, and if these were breached the castle fell to the invader. A castle keep (the innermost stronghold, often a tower) was not designed for a last line of defense as in the case of European castles. Walls were built of stone, but the donjon, or keep, was of timber. Most of the castles standing today have been reconstructed at some time or other.

Japanese castles were built to impress and to symbolize the power of the *daimyo* who resided within. The facade was designed to inspire fear or admiration; thus, many of the castles are very beautiful and awe-inspiring.

One of the best known and most beautiful castles in Japan is the Himeji Castle about 20 miles (32 km) east of Osaka. It was acquired in 1609 by Ikeda Terumasa, the trusted son-in-law of Shogun Tokugawa Ieyasu, as a defense against the western lords. Its towers, with their curving roofs and white walls rising above the heavy gray stone walls, are a magnificent sight. The castle gives the impression of impregnable solidity, yet has elegant and graceful lines. Its other name, White Heron Castle, is apt; it has the appearance of a great white bird, or a flock of white birds, in flight.

In contrast, about 15 miles (24 km) east of Himeji Castle, are the ruins of Okayama Castle. Completely black, it is known as the Crow Castle. It was built in 1573, and only two turrets of the original structure remain.

Osaka Castle is steeped in history. This large, majestic-looking structure reflects the ambitions and prestige of Shogun Toyotomi Hideyoshi, who built the original castle between 1583 and 1586 with the labor of 630,000 men. Given a strategic position, the castle was 1.7 miles (2.7 km) long and 1.2 miles (1.9 km) wide.

In 1615 Osaka Castle was besieged and burned by Tokugawa Ieyasu, who seized the shogunate from Hideyoshi's son. Ieyasu ordered that all traces of the old castle be demolished and a new one built according to a completely new plan. He wanted to eradicate the symbols left by Hideyoshi and build a castle to stand as a symbol of his own power to the lords of the far west.

The new castle was smaller and did not include the outermost moats of the original. Fires and a brief civil war in 1867 finally destroyed it. The present structure is a modern 1931 concrete replica, which includes some towers built in 1620.

Plan of Himeji Castle showing:
1 Main citadel
2-5 Citadel
6 Main donjon or keep
7 Inner moat
8-18 Gates
19 Water gate 1
20 Water gate 2
21 Gate
22 Moat

Whisper on the verandah by Harunobu.

POETRY

Poetry is not the exclusive preserve of intellectuals. Poems appear in newspapers regularly, and most Japanese write poems without being embarrassed about it. It is one of the nation's living arts.

Poetry began as the language of the aristocrats. Emperor Meiji is said to have written 100,000 poems. Often, poetry was the only communication between secret lovers. Messages were dispatched with some small symbolic token—a leaf or a fan.

HAIKU Classical Japanese poetry concentrates on distilling a thought in the briefest and most beautiful way. The poet tends to hint and suggest. Here is such a poem by Matsuo Basho (1614–1694):

Kare eda ni	On a withered dry branch
karasu no tomarikeri	a crow stops and rests;
aki no kure.	autumn dusk.

The main forms used were called *waka* ("wah-kah"); *tanka* ("tah-n-kah"), or short poem; and *haiku* ("hie-koo"), or very short poem. The *haiku* is a very popular form. There are strict rules of composition. Basho's poem on the crow is a *haiku*. It is not easy to write *haiku* with its tight line limitations. Nor is *haiku* easy to understand, because of complex nuances. As in many art forms, constraints bring out some of the finest work.

SENRYU AND ACROSTIC The *senryu* ("sehn-ree-you") is a special type of *haiku*. Comic or frivolous, like the limerick, it gives poetry a humorous side.

> After he's scolded   Now the man has a child
> His wife too much,   He knows all the names
> He cooks the rice.   Of the local dogs.

The poets themselves sometimes imposed additional constraints. It showed finesse to send one's lover an acrostic poem, where the first letters of every line spell a word.

> *I*n the capital is the one I love, like
> *R*obes of stuff so precious, yet now threadbare.
> *I* have come far on this journey,
> *S*ad and tearful are my thoughts.
> — from the *Ise Monogatari*

RENGA The *renga* ("rehn-gah"), or linked poem, was a game, an intellectual challenge. One person wrote two or three lines, the next another two, and so on. Rules controlled not only syllables; there were also patterns to be followed, such as the second verse should mention this or that and the moon should come up in the *n*th verse, but only once, etc. Practice sharpened the minds and sensitivities of the great poets.

MODERN POETRY After the Meiji Restoration in the 19th century, the influence of European free verse caused major changes in poetic forms. A nation of highly disciplined poets showed that in spite of the confines of their past, individuality could break through. Here are two examples:

My nails are cut
My manicure is done
My blouse is ironed
My shoes are polished
And now,
I only go to your funeral.
— Takata Kyoko

Going into the room,
You hesitate, standing for a while.
It's lemon.
You notice.
There's pain.

Eventually you find the wound.

This is the frightening thing;
that in every part of time, there's a delay.
— Kitamura Taro

HISTORICAL NOVELS

Classical Japanese prose began in the Heian period (A.D. 794–1185), and was mainly the work of women. This period also saw the development of the *kana* scripts, which opened the way to easier writing. Major works produced then included *Tosa Diary, Taketori Tales, Tales of Ise, Utsubo Tales,* and the two classics, *The Tale of Genji* and the *Pillow Book.*

The Tale of Genji, written about A.D. 1000 by Lady Murasaki Shikibu, is perhaps the Heian work with the greatest influence on Japanese literature. Generations of Japanese scholars have read and dissected this tale of fiction woven around Lady Murasaki's realistic and minute observations of court life. It is a unique kind of novel, having nothing dramatic, unnatural, or improbable in it. The style is ornate and indirect.

The Pillow Book, or *Pillow Sketches,* of Sei Shonagon is another outstanding work by a Japanese woman. It introduced an open and easy style and revealed the author's opinions and feelings. The book's postscript is typical of her style:

> It has become too dark for literary work, and my pen is worn out. I will bring these sketches to a close. They are a record of that which I have seen with my eyes and felt with my heart, not written that others might read them, but put together to solace the loneliness of my home life. When I think how I tried to keep them secret, conscious of vulgar and exaggerated remarks which have escaped me, the tears flow uncontrollably.
>
> — from *The Pillow Book*

A section of *The Tale of Genji* picture scroll, which is considered a masterpiece in its own right. It is believed to have been produced in the early 12th century.

97

DECLINE AND REVIVAL OF LITERATURE

Toward the end of the Heian period, and in the Kamakura period that followed, several major written works dealt with historical subjects: *Eiga Monogatari, O-Kagami, Gempei Seisuiki, Heike Monogatari. Monogatari* ("moh-noh-gah-tah-ree") means tale or narrative.

Japanese literature declined in the Kamakura period, reaching its lowest point by the end of the Muromachi period (1338-1573). Intellectuals turned to China, as is reflected in the literature and social codes. Women were thrust out of public life in conformity with Chinese thinking.

The Tokugawa period (1600-1867) saw great changes in the literary scene. The printing press had been introduced, script and grammar simplified, and vocabulary expanded. Writers began to address both the aristocrats and the common people. There was a new "Japaneseness" developing—a break from Chinese cultural millstones, although a great many Chinese words were absorbed at this time. It was in this period that the great *haiku* poets, including Basho, wrote their masterpieces.

"Sora bidding farewell to Basho."

Among the writers of the Tokugawa period are Ihara Saikaku (1642–1693) with his style of realism and humor reminiscent of *The Tale of Genji* and *Pillow Book;* Kiokutei Bakin (1767–1848), who wrote what is perhaps the most famous novel after *The Tale of Genji,* the *Hakkuden;* and Jippensha Ikku (d. 1831), author of a humorous novel, *Hizakurige,* that has been compared to Charles Dickens' *The Pickwick Papers.*

MODERN LITERATURE

After the Meiji Restoration, when Japan set out to catch up with 200 years of Western development, there was an explosion of fiction writing. It was a vigorous growth both in terms of volume and a blossoming of Japan's finest writers.

The Japanese read voraciously, not just for knowledge but mainly for pleasure. Today, Japan has the highest ratio of novels printed per capita in the world. There is a large book market for popular romances and thrillers, as well as historical novels.

Modern Japanese writers explore styles and themes quite different from those of past novels. They have become greatly absorbed in the psychology of the characters; in this, they resemble Western writers. Yet there is a special Japanese slant always present, reflecting the Japanese mind today, a mixture of tradition and individuality.

Women novelists have always held a significant position in Japanese fiction. Enchi Fumiko, born in 1895, is in a class of her own among modern women writers. Her books span the era of major change in Japanese literature. Conscious of the suppression of Japanese women over the last 600 years, she has written many stories on that theme. *Onnazaka (The Waiting Years)* took her eight years to complete and won a top prize in the Japanese literary world.

Kawabata Yasunari (1899–1972) was the first Japanese to be awarded the Nobel Prize, in 1968, for his novel, *Snow Country*. In 1994 writer Oe Kenzaburo (born 1935) was also awarded the Nobel Prize for Literature. Mishima Yukio (1925–1970), one of the best known in the West today, was an intellectual of very strong opinions. His novels deal with the more sordid aspects of life, but his contribution to world literature is undeniable. He killed himself by committing *seppuku* in public in 1970.

Natsume Soseki was one of the first post-Restoration writers (1867–1916) educated in the West. His best-known books are *Botchan*, *I am a Cat*, and *The Heart of Things*. His portrait is found on the Japanese 1,000 yen banknote.

The stage set of a *noh* theater is usually sparse, but this is more than compensated for by the splendid costumes of lead actors. Musicians sit to one side of the stage.

JAPANESE THEATER

Japanese theater, which is always intertwined with dance and music, began in the seventh century A.D. with Shinto ritualistic dances. These dances are still performed today in essentially the same form. *Noh* drama, which developed in the 14th century, is one of the main branches of Japanese theater.

NOH *Noh* plays are a mixture of dance and drama based on Shinto dances and Buddhist teachings. The subject matter includes the sin of killing, the afterlife, the transience of the material world, the power of Buddha, and the evil power of lust. In spite of the seriousness underlying the themes, Noh is a visual delight, the costumes are colorful, made of silver and gold brocade, and elaborately embroidered.

The action on stage is in the form of "flashbacks" from the memories of the characters. They are obscure, idyllic, and lyrical, and the script is heavy with allusion and symbolism. The dialogue—archaic phrases in chanted tones—is incomprehensible to present-day audiences, and even educated Japanese need a script to follow the play.

Noh started as an amusement performed in temple grounds for the people, but the aristocracy adopted it as their private theater, and in the Tokugawa period legally deprived the masses of *noh*. Only warriors were allowed to watch *noh* performances, although, because of its Buddhist influence, *noh* seldom included warrior roles.

"The art of allusion, or this love of allusion in art, is the root of the noh.*"*

— *Ezra Pound, a scholar and interpreter of* noh.

Noh reached its peak in the 15th century, declined, and was revived in the early 20th century. A traditional *noh* theater program would include five *noh* plays with three or four *kyogen* ("kee-yoh-gehn") plays in between.

KYOGEN *Kyogen* is a comic interlude. The word means "mad words," and as in *noh*, the performers are all men. *Kyogen* reveals many different and significant facets of Japanese character.

Kyogen plays were originally performed in temples to relieve the strain of prolonged Buddhist services. They are short, very humorous, and never involve more than three characters. About a third of the themes are of a servant mocking his feudal lord. The lord is made to look ridiculous but is eventually proven right. Another third or so of *kyogen* themes poke fun at Buddhism, even though Buddhism was then the religion of the aristocracy and it was in Buddhist temples that *kyogen* was performed.

The costumes of *kyogen* are those of the 15th century, but the language is the language of the 17th century: *kyogen*, unlike *noh*, was passed down from generation to generation orally and only written down in the 17th century.

A temple attendant performs a ritual dance in a Shinto temple. Japanese theater began on the grounds of temples and the dances performed on stage today have not changed much from the original forms.

Young people are trained for a festival dance item. Dancing is not as enthusiastically encouraged as are music and art.

KABUKI The three *kanji* that make up *kabuki* mean song, dance, and skill. In its heyday, *kabuki* attracted thousands on every performance. *Kabuki* flowered in the Genroku era (1688–1704) when great novelists and poets like Basho were bringing a new impetus to the arts. Japan's greatest playwright, Chikamatsu Monzaemon (1653–1724), was in his prime, and the first of a dynasty of actors started: the Danjuro line. *Kabuki* reached its peak in the 18th century.

Kabuki is melodramatic and spectacular. Climaxes require a special look called the *mie* ("mee-eh"): to the accompaniment of wooden clappers, the actor strikes a grandiose pose, widening his eyes, and crossing one of them. Unlike *noh*, which always has the same backdrop of a painting of a pine tree, *kabuki* has elaborate props like trapdoors and a revolving stage. A close rapport exists between actors and audience, aided by a walkway that extends into the audience. Actors address some lines to the audience, members of which shout their comments as the play progresses.

Kabuki plots revolve around the elevation of a commoner to a higher status, people changing forms, incredible swordfights, lovers' suicides, and a terrible Japanese insult—slapping someone with a slipper or clog.

BUNRAKU *Bunraku,* the puppet theater, developed from storytelling into a musical form in the 16th century. Storytelling is still very popular in Japan. Every television station devotes at least an hour a day to the traditional half-recited, half-sung style of storytelling.

Today, puppets are mechanically complicated figures about 3 feet (1 m) high. To operate one puppet requires three men. The puppeteers are not hidden, but as soon as the play begins, the audience ceases to notice the puppeteers.

MUSIC

Japanese music, like many aspects of the theatrical arts, has Chinese origins. The Chinese three-stringed fiddle, in particular, had a major influence on Japanese music. It produces sounds quite different from those produced by the Japanese lute. Music is inextricably linked with dance and, through dance, the theater.

With the opening of Japan to the rest of the world, the Japanese absorbed all forms of Western music with great fervor and no cultural conflicts whatsoever. Traditional Japanese music ceased to develop from about the 18th century

Bunraku or puppet theater. The puppet is manipulated by two or three men who are visible to the audience. The people covered completely in black in the back are the puppetteers' assistants.

LEISURE

WITH THE INTERNATIONALIZING OF LEISURE via television and recorded music, Japanese styles of leisure have become similar to those in North America and Europe. They have absorbed pop music and adopted baseball with as widespread and intense an enthusiasm as one sees in the United States. Golf is the hobby of the upper class; tennis and skiing are the craze of the majority.

The sports craze is not wholly due to pleasure-seeking. It has become a necessity because, along with other things, many Japanese have adopted a Western-style diet. Once on a low-calorie diet of tofu, seafood, and miso soup, many are now eating fattening amounts of junk food, and therefore have to spend time exercising to work off the calories.

A new feature found in cities such as Tokyo is the indoor sports club. To cater to several sports interests, and because of space constraints, such clubs are housed in multistory buildings.

There, for membership fees varying from as little as US$480 a year to as much as US$6,700, and a nominal entrance fee, the Japanese can swim laps, play indoor baseball or racket games such as squash or badminton, work out in a gymnasium, and perhaps even play a few holes of golf. Then, after the exercise, they can relax in a sauna and indulge in a snack— all under one roof.

Below: **Nearly all schools in Japan have their own baseball team. Baseball programs are top-rated on television, and some Japanese teams have American players. The game was first played in Japan in 1873.**

Opposite: **The Japanese are a nature-loving people. Picnics and outings are popular in spring and summer.**

Above: **One is never too young to use a camera. Cameras are carried everywhere, to shrines and other places in Japan, as well as abroad, for the Japanese are avid photographers.**

Opposite, top: **Inside a pachinko parlor.**

TRAVEL, READING, AND PACHINKO

Japanese travel a lot, but mostly in organized groups. They have a passion for photography; whether abroad or at home, the Japanese photograph almost anything they see.

Reading newspapers, magazines, or novels is another passion. *Manga* ("mahn-gah"), or comics, have become a national craze in recent years, and range from the pornographic to Shakespeare's plays, from funny to serious. The Japanese seem to read them everywhere. Restaurants provide stacks of *manga* for their customers to peruse, and truck drivers keep a *manga* on the seat beside them for a quick read at breaks along the journey.

At night, the night spots and bars all over Japan ring with the same guffaws and boisterous behavior as all over the world. Japanese drink regularly, although many Westerners believe that their capacity to hold liquor is low.

One of the more unusual leisure pursuits in Japan is *pachinko* ("pah-chin-koh"), the pinball machine. In the cities, thousands of businessmen and workers stand side by side, pushing levers to set the balls moving, apparently oblivious to their surroundings. *Pachinko* is a mindless activity and the prizes are insignificant. Yet, it has been reported that 15 million people, mostly men, spend more than $3 billion a year on this game, which

they play daily, in many cases for hours on end. It is a form of escapism, like drinking and reading comics.

There are still traditional Japanese facets to their leisure. The appreciation of the ancient is alive and strong in the Japanese. Families travel around Japan to see the old temples, castles, rock gardens, and the famous scenic spots. It is not just aesthetic appreciation; there is a nationalistic pride in all this.

In a nation that has the second largest economy in the world after the United States (as of 2001), relatively simple housing, and a lack of ostentatious consumption like that of the West, the amount of money spent on leisure activities is unusually high.

JAPANESE BATHS

Bathing is a very important daily activity to the Japanese. The word for bath—*O-furo*—is given the honorific prefix *O*.

The Japanese have no qualms about showing their naked bodies. Public baths in the country are still places where men and women bathe together. They start by washing every part of the body meticulously, often asking a friend or acquaintance to scrub their backs. Having made sure that they are clean, they get into the bath-pool or bathtub and sit in it, soaking in the heat of very hot water for a long time.

Japan's turbulent past gave rise to a warrior class, skilled in the art of weaponry and hand-to-hand combat. Modern sports derived from ancient arts of warfare have taken away none of the skill, flexibility, speed, or tenacity of combat, but they have added rules for judging tournaments in judo (top), kendo, or fencing (center), and sumo wrestling (bottom).

FESTIVALS

FESTIVALS, called *matsuri* ("maht-soo-ree"), are major social events in Japan. Whether religious, superstitious, or rooted in ancient events that are now irrelevant, they allow the disciplined Japanese to relax and let their hair down.

NEW YEAR FESTIVAL

New Year's Day, January 1, is celebrated nationwide. Businesses close and family reunions are held. Three bamboo and pine branches are put up in front of the house and a rope stretched across the gate. In the living room, decorative rice cakes, seaweed, dried sardines, persimmons, oranges, and a lobster with evergreens or ferns, are placed on a special stand. *Zoni* ("zoh-nee"), a soup of pounded rice cakes, vegetables, and fish or chicken, is eaten. *Toso* ("toh-soh"), a special spiced *sake,* is drunk, and a stack of trays called *jubako* ("joo-bah-koh"), or "stacked-up boxes" is packed with tidbits for visitors.

It is a day for visiting the local shrine and for calling on one's friends and relatives; these days, it could be a day to sit in front of the television set because excellent traditional programs are broadcast on New Year's Day.

January 2 in many ways is regarded as the first day of the year. One does one's first calligraphy, writes the first poem, plays the first musical piece, sews the first stitches, and gathers sentimental treasures around the pillow to ensure the first dream of the year is happy. Tradesmen used to decorate carts gaily before setting out on the first business day.

The festival ends on January 7, when a rice porridge seasoned with seven herbs is eaten. Other events, such as the poetry reading at the emperor's poetry party on January 18, draw the festivities out a little longer.

Opposite: **The Gion Festival originated in Kyoto, but it is now also celebrated in other parts of Japan. Here, men in costume carry a float through Kyoto's main street.**

Tanabata in Sendai is one
of the great festivals of
Japan's northeast. Main
streets are decorated and
several million people
visit Sendai to take part in
the event.

TANABATA

The Tanabata festival's origin is in a Chinese story of two stars. Vega, or the weaver star, fell in love with Altair, the cowherd, and in the whirlwind of their honeymoon, they neglected their duties. Angry with the lovers, the god of the firmament separated them. On the seventh night of the seventh month every year, the legend goes, magpies form a bridge across the celestial river dividing them (the Milky Way), but the lovers can only be reunited if it does not rain, and the river is narrow enough.

On July 7 this romance is symbolized by bamboo cuttings set up in each house. They are decorated with poems on strips of different-colored paper that are later dropped into a river. At Sendai, thousands of folk dancers in light summer *kimono* and flower-decorated straw hats dance through the town after dark.

BON

The purpose of the Bon, or O-Bon, festival originally was to offer prayers and perform ritual dances in the Buddhist month when ghosts of the dead were believed to return to Earth. From this 14th century custom it has become a summer festival of dancing and lanterns.

Candles and floating lanterns on rivers and lakes (supplemented by fireworks these days) guide the spirits back to the paradise or hell they came from. In temples and graveyards flickering lights bring an air of quiet eeriness and subdued festivity.

In village squares towers are set up where drummers, and perhaps a band, pound out an all-night rhythm, pacing the feet and hand movements of hundreds of ordinary folk dancing in concentric circles around the towers, repeating the same simple movements for hours on end, trancelike.

In China's remote past, dolls were part of the ritual cleansing of ill fortune. Paper dolls were made and given the owner's bad luck, then cast into rivers or lakes. Japan's Hinamatsuri may have begun for the same reason, but the dolls today are far too valuable to throw away.

HINAMATSURI

This festival is really girls' day in Japan, a day when girls get to play with beautiful dolls that are works of fine craftsmanship. The family's treasured doll collection is brought out and displayed on tiered shelves for about two weeks. There are usually more than ten dolls; the emperor and empress dolls are put on the top shelf, their courtiers below them. The doll display is often accompanied by an equally exquisite display of miniature furniture and food.

Special sweets are eaten, and the girls of the family play hostess to the friends who visit them to admire the dolls. Hinamatsuri is their day.

Above: **Costumes and pageantry—sometimes bizarre, always colorful—mark the Toshogu shrine grand festival.**

Opposite: **Carried, pushed or, in this case, pulled, the floats make their way through the main streets during the Gion Festival.**

TOSHOGU SHRINE FESTIVAL

This is a Shinto religious extravaganza. It is said to commemorate the death of Tokugawa Ieyasu, one of the three warlords who molded Japan into a single homogenous country. Three movable shrines are carried around the Toshogu shrine in Nikko, Tochigi Prefecture, where a procession of a thousand march dressed in Tokugawa period costumes. They are accompanied by a motley crowd of followers dressed as monkeys, lions, *samurai*, falconers, and fairies.

There is something for everyone: religious shrine dances, other special dances performed by Buddhist priests, and even a demonstration of mounted archery.

DAIMONJI

Every year, as the O-Bon celebrations of the month of ghosts culminate in a night of bonfires and lanterns all over Japan, residents of Kyoto and the surrounding district settle down to watch Mount Nyoigatake. At 8 P.M. on August 16, a bonfire starts burning on the mountain slope and slowly spreads out to form the character *dai* ("dah-ee"), meaning big. *Dai* resembles a man with arms and legs stretched out. The bonfires cover an area of about 12,000 square yards (10,000 square m). *Daimonji* ("dah-ee-mon-jee") means a large-character fire.

Soon fires start burning on other hills, each in the form of the character, *dai*. It is a spectacular finale to the month of festivities for visiting ghosts from other worlds.

GION MATSURI

On July 17 the ancient and dignified city of Kyoto, with its beautiful temples and serene parks and gardens of mosses and rocks, erupts into a brilliant spectacle. The Gion Matsuri brings color and music, gaiety and open friendliness. From 9 A.M. to 11 A.M., 29 carved or gilded floats, decorated with tapestries, gongs, flutes, and drums, are carried or drawn through the town in a procession. Old family houses and old stores throw open their doors, displaying their treasures and family heirlooms.

Everyone is out to enjoy themselves. There is an almost Latin fiesta atmosphere that contrasts with the festival's origins in A.D. 869, when the people of Kyoto took to the streets to pray for divine protection against an epidemic that was sweeping across the country.

BOYS' DAY

On the fifth day of the fifth month, Japanese boys have their special day. Mounted on poles at almost every house, brightly colored carp-shaped banners of paper or cloth flutter in the wind like flags or runway air-socks. Five hundred years ago, these were first put up to frighten away the swarms of May insects.

A tiered stand in every house displays the family collection of warrior figures and instruments of war: perhaps an antique family sword, a silk banner of the family crest, or a set of spears. Nowadays, May 5 is also celebrated as Children's Day, but the older tradition lingers, of wishing the boys of the family health and the courage and fortitude of *samurai*.

KUROFUNE MATSURI

The Japanese celebrate Commodore Perry's landing at Shimada on the Izu Peninsula. *Kuro* ("koo-roh") means "black" and *fune* ("foo-nay") means "ship." The black, tarred hulls of U.S. naval ships in Perry's time made a menacing impression on the Japanese, who did not paint the hulls of their boats. In spite of the unwelcome intrusion of the Americans in 1857, the Kurofune festival commemorates the event with a historical pageant every year around May 17. There is also a US naval parade.

AOI MATSURI

The Aoi Matsuri is said to be the oldest festival celebrated in the world. From the sixth century A.D., this pageant of color, costumes, and music from flutes, gongs, and drums, has snaked its way annually through the streets of Kyoto. The Hollyhock festival, as it is sometimes known, is celebrated on May 15, between the last of the cherry blossoms and the first irises.

The highlight is the imperial procession, reenacted these days in the dress of the Heian period with the imperial oxcart, its lacquer beautifully preserved and its wheels squeaking to attest to its authenticity. Brocaded *kimono* with huge sleeves, sprays of artificial wisteria, little black hats perched on top of the attendants' heads, ornate saddles, enormously impractical umbrellas decorated with flowers, and a seemingly endless array of strange and colorful costumes all combine to make the Aoi festival a dazzling spectacle.

The imperial oxcart is brought out for the Aoi festival in Kyoto. Kyoto became the capital of Japan in the 8th century.

The kite battle of the Hamamatsu festival is held over three days, and the entire city turns up for the event. Each kite bears a neighborhood insignia, and the object of the fight is to bring down kites belonging to other neighborhoods.

HAMAMATSU MATSURI

The Suwa shrine festival at Hamamatsu in Shizuoka is not just another shrine festival. It includes the *Hamamatsu Odakoage*: the big-kite fight at Nakatajima beach. This festival began about 1550, when a feudal lord announced the name of his newborn son by flying a large kite with the child's name on it.

Today, up to 60 teams from different districts manipulate giant kites with unbelievable agility, skill, and intense excitement, trying to cut each other's kite string with the abrasive strings of their own kites. The festival is a tumult of shouting, leaping, jostling, and laughing—a riot of color and splendor with all the tension of a football game and the gaiety of an outdoor springtime party.

HAKONE TORII MATSURI

This is the festival for travelers celebrated by the lake of Ashinoko (also known as Lake Ashi and Lake Hakone) in the mountains south of Tokyo. The Torii Matsuri originated from casting little paper replicas of *torii* (gateway structures) into the lake to ensure safety when traveling. It has become a glittering spectacle. A life-size *torii,* decorated with 1,000 lanterns, is set afloat on the lake and burned.

TENJIN MATSURI

The Tenjin Matsuri of Osaka is one of the greatest and most dazzling of the festivals of Japan. It began when the people of Osaka brought to Temmangu shrine pieces of paper cut into human form as offerings against the diseases that spread in the summer heat. These paper offerings were then carried down to the river and thrown into the water.

Today, the festival is centered around a magnificent evening procession that starts on land from Temmangu shrine and moves down to floats drifting on the river. Bonfires are lit on the riverbanks as night falls. The procession is led by six frenzied men beating on a 5-foot (1.5-meter) diameter drum as if possessed. They are followed by a scarlet-robed horseman, dancers with spinning umbrellas, an oxcart bearing books, boxes of rice offerings, palanquins, portable shrines, a lion dance, and, to ensure that dozens of proud parents will share the joy of the day, streams of powdered, rouged, and prettied-up children.

SHIRAOI-NO-IOMANTE

This is a solemn hunting festival of the Ainu, the aboriginal people of Japan who now live only in Hokkaido. The Iomante, or bear festival, originated from the sacrificial killing of a baby bear specially raised for the annual event. It was believed that the spirit of the bear went up to heaven.

The baby bear is no longer sacrificed but a hideous, grotesque thing, almost like a face from a science fiction fantasy, represents the bear.

BUDDHA'S BIRTHDAY

Buddha's birthday is celebrated in Buddhist temples all over Japan with the *Kanbutsu* ("kahn-boot-tsoo") ceremony, the baptizing of Buddha. It was first performed at the Genkoji temple, Yamato, in A.D. 606.

In the temple grounds, an image of the infant Buddha is set up under a roof decorated with flowers; this is the *hanamido,* temple of flowers. The priests give worshipers a sweet tea made from hydrangea leaves to take home.

Buddha's birthday has thus come to be associated with flowers, and in Hibiya Park, Tokyo, thousands of flower-bearing Buddhist children march in procession.

IZUMO-TAISHA JINZAISAI

In the tenth month of the lunar calendar, all the gods in Japan are believed to gather at Izumo Taisha Shrine. In Izumo, the month is called *Kamiarizuki* ("kah-mee-ah-ree-zoo-kee")—"the month when the gods are present"—and everywhere else it is called *Kannazuki* ("kah-nah-zoo-kee")—"the month when the gods are absent." The gods are welcomed at the seashore with a rite. The procession then makes its way toward the shrine.

NAMAHAGE

Namahage is celebrated at the Akagami shrine of Oga city, in Akita Prefecture. It is a strange mixture of a harvest festival and an orgy of scaring children into obedience throughout the coming year.

After prayers in front of a bonfire, young unmarried men dressed in frightening masks, straw cloaks, and trousers with bells around their waists, go from house to house. Sometimes they carry a wooden pail and a wooden replica of a kitchen knife, knock on doors, and ask, "Is there any wicked person in this house?" They are invited in and offered rice cakes and *sake*, and move on, chuckling and getting more and more drunk.

CHAKKIRAKO

Held every January 15 in Kanagawa prefecture, Chakkirako is an ancient dance performed by young girls dressed in *haregi*, meaning best *kimono*. The name of the festival represents the sound of the *ayadake* ("ah-yah-dah-kay"), a paper-wrapped bamboo percussion instrument, similar to castanets, that the dancers carry.

Many young children are frightened by the evil-looking masks the "devil" bachelors wear during Namahage.

119

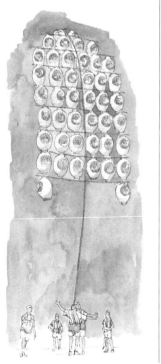

HANAGASA-ODORI

This is one of the great festivals of Tohoku, celebrated at Yamagata at the beginning of August. The *hanagasa* is a hat on which flowers are painted.

The *hanagasa* dance overwhelms one by the sheer numbers—thousands of girls, swinging their hats first in circles in a steady rhythm to the music above their heads, then almost down to their knees, cry out, in unison, *"Yassho! Makasho! Yassho! Makasho!"*

DEER-DANCE FESTIVAL

This is a delightful fall festival of Ehime province. Young boys dressed in tubular armless robes with deer-head masks, complete with antlers, beat small drums as they step and sway in a graceful dance, searching for the "doe" hiding from them. At the Awatsuhiko shrine, Awajima, Ehime, a very special eight-deer dance, the *Yatsushishi-odori* ("yaht-zoo-she-she oh-door-ri"), is particularly well-known. (*Odori* means "dance.")

Deer dances, *Shika-odori*, have been performed at fall festivals in Ehime since the 17th century.

CALENDAR OF JAPANESE FESTIVALS*

Festival	Date	Place	Description
New Year	Jan 1–7	Pan-Japan	
Iwate Snow festival	Feb 3–12	Tohoku	Ice sculptures
Hinamatsuri	Mar 3	Pan-Japan	Dolls
Kasuga Matsuri	Mar 3	Nara	Lanterns
Buddha's Birthday	Apr 8		Procession
Fire-walking	Apr 15	Miyajima	Includes Bugaku, an ancient dance of Central Asia, seen only in Japan
Green Day	Apr 30	Pan-Japan	Environmental day
Hamamatsu festival	May 3–5	Shizuoka	Big-kite fights
Boys' Day	May 5	Pan-Japan	Carp streamers
Aoi Matsuri (Hollyhock festival)	May 15	Shimogamo Kamigamo	Imperial procession, flower decorated umbrellas
Toshogu Shrine Grand Festival	May 17	Nikko	Tokugawa period pageant, archery
Takigi-Noh	Jun 1–3	Kyoto	
Gion Matsuri	Jul 17	Kyoto	Floats
Nomaoi	Jul 22–25	Kyoto	Wild horse chasing
Bon	Jul 13–16 Aug 12–16	Pan-Japan Kyoto	Floating lanterns, fireworks
Black Ship festival, Kurofune Matsuri	Jul 8 May 19-21	Kurihama Shimoda	Historical pageant
Tenjin Matsuri	Jul 26	Osaka	Procession—land and river
Tanabata (Star festival)	Aug 7	Sendai	Bamboo branches with colored paper ornaments and love poems
Hanagasa-odori	Aug 5-7	Yamagata	
Bonbori Matsuri	Aug 6-9	Kamakura	Lanterns
Daimonji bonfire	Aug 16	Kyoto	Bonfires in character "Dai"
Kokeshi festival	First weekend of Sept.	Miyagi	Costume parade, dances, memorial service for imperfect dolls destroyed the year before
Shiraoi Dosanko Winter Festival (Shiraoi Iomante)	First weekend of Feb.	Hokkaido	

Dates are approximate

121

FOOD

IN TASTE, AND ABOVE ALL IN PRESENTATION, Japanese food reflects the character and culture of the Japanese. It is a low-protein diet based on rice and, to a lesser degree, noodles. The main sources of protein are fish and soybeans. The flavorings are generally subtle, with sugar and soy sauce their main ingredients.

Food is always presented to please the eye and whet the appetite. It has been said that the Japanese "eat with their eyes." Meals were served on a variety of differently shaped dishes long before the West broke from their rigid limitation of round plates. There are many rules of presentation; for instance, a whole fish is always placed before the guest with its head facing left.

STAPLES

Although rice is the main carbohydrate, noodles are often eaten. The range of noodle dishes varies from the thick *udon* ("oo-don") to the very fine *soba* ("soh-bah") noodles. *Soba* is sometimes eaten cold dipped in a sweet soy sauce with finely chopped scallions floating in it. In a unique food-and-fun festival event, noodles in a soup are poured down a bamboo trough. Hungry eaters line the sides of the trough and use chopsticks to gobble and suck in the noodles as they flow past.

A popular and unusual carbohydrate is the tuber *konnyaku* ("kon-nyah-koo"). It is believed to have come from Indonesia and now grows in a limited area in Japan. *Konnyaku* is eaten raw, boiled, or reconstituted from *konnyaku* flour.

Yam, which the Japanese call "mountain potato," is another favorite. Fried in batter or steamed, the yam appears frequently in Japanese dishes.

Opposite: Men and women enjoy a warm dish of *oden* (oh-den), pieces of radish, fish cake, and other traditional foods broiled in a special soup, along with beer or *sake*. Street stalls such as this one are extremely popular as an after work gathering place for small crowds of working men and women.

Below: Japanese eat sticky rice, which can be picked up in lumps with their pointed chopsticks. They pick up a piece of vegetable or meat, dip it in a sauce, and put it in their mouths. Then they eat a mouthful of rice. They generally do not place the morsels of meat and vegetables on top of their rice.

FISH IS THEIR FORTE

Fish is prepared grilled on a steel plate called a *teppan* ("tay-pahn"), cooked with soy sauce, or made into fish cakes and fish balls. Dried and fermented fish or *bonito* ("boh-ni-toh"), known as *katsuo-bushi* ("kaht-zoo-oh boo-she"), is used to make *miso shiru* ("mee-soh shee-roo"), or soybean paste soup, and shavings of it are used as a garnish.

The Japanese love raw fish, *sashimi* ("sah-shee-mee"), an expensive delicacy eaten with *wasabi* ("wah-sah-bee"), or Japanese horseradish. Fish is more common in *sushi* ("soo-shee"), little pieces of raw fish on one-mouthful lumps of rice seasoned with vinegar.

The origin of *sushi* is interesting. Transportation of fresh sea fish inland was slow, and a sour fermented rice and fish mixture was eaten to mask the decaying fish smell. When fermentation was discontinued, vinegar was added to maintain the essential flavor. Now only the freshest fish is used.

FISH BELIEFS Most Japanese observe some form of fish calendar: when to eat salmon, trout, tuna, etc. The first *bonito* of the season is highly prized. The Japanese have many "fish" theories: one concerns the *sanma* ("sahn-mah"), a fish not widely eaten elsewhere, which is supposed to cure various ills. It is said "when the *sanma* comes, the masseurs go away."

Fish is also often mentioned in poetry and comic verse. Fish appear in various emblems, such as the carp-shaped banners put up on the boys' festival day.

OTHER SEAFOOD Japanese eat other seafood, including seaweed. Seaweed is a major source of minerals and other trace elements, such as iodine, in their diet. Eels are a specialty. *Kabayaki* ("kah-bah-yah-kee")— grilled eel—is a mouthwatering dish. The eel is steamed first and then grilled dark brown and placed on top of a bowl of rice.

An interesting prawn was discovered by accident when a fisherman made a mistake in lowering his nets and drew up a pinkish transparent prawn never before seen. The Japanese call it the *sakura ebi* ("sah-koo-rah eh-bee"), or "cherry blossom prawn," because of its color.

SUSHI

Sushi is not restricted to raw fish. Hundreds of variants exist that use different tidbits with the rice, including cucumber, cooked egg, steamed prawns, raw cuttlefish, seaweed, and shellfish.

Sushi is presented in bite-sized pieces. One picks up a piece, turns it over and around, dips the top in a saucer of soy sauce with pungent *wasabi*, and then pops the whole morsel into one's mouth. This is a little tricky at first.

MEAT

Pork came to Kyushu from China via Korea, and the best pork dishes are thus found in the south. A pork chop dish called *tonkatsu* ("tohn-kat-zu") and other specialties exist, but in general pork has not developed into a major food item in Japan.

The window display is the menu. Plastic dishes of items on the menu, with prices in some cases, help customers decide what to eat or what suits their budget before entering the restaurant.

Japanese eat beef only in special dishes. *Sukiyaki* ("soo-key-yahk-key")*,* thin strips of meat cooked with vegetables at the table, is one such dish. It is delicious made with *Kobe* ("koh-bay") beef, a highly marbled beef. Cattle are fattened and massaged so that fat is dispersed evenly throughout the muscle. This gives the beef a tender, melt-in-the-mouth quality. *Kobe* beef is probably the most expensive beef in the world.

Venison is one of Japan's more unusual meats. The best venison is believed to come from Hokkaido, where the deer supposedly eat grasses with medicinal properties.

The Japanese also eat horsemeat because they enjoy the uncommon taste and texture. It is sometimes eaten raw as *sashimi.*

VEGETABLES

Japanese vegetables include those well-known in Europe and Asia, such as spinach and eggplant, as well as a variety of flowers, stems, and roots. Vegetables that are unfamiliar in the West are *fuki* ("foo-key"), a butter-bur; *gobo* (goh-boe), a burdock; *daikon* ("dye-con"), a kind of radish; and even chrysanthemum leaves. *Daikon,* especially when thinly sliced or grated, is seen in most Japanese meals as an individual dish, a pickle, or garnish.

Vegetable vendors materialize magically during festivals. These flimsy structures are obviously temporary and are located near temple grounds. Spiritual and practical concerns are thus conveniently dealt with.

EGGS

The Japanese have their own ways of handling eggs. *Chawan-mushi* ("chah-wahn moo-she")—literally steamed in a cup—are steamed, whipped eggs with tasty additions. In cities, the *okonomiyakiya* ("oh-koh-noh-mee-yah-kee-yah")—omelette shops—provide the customer with a staggering choice of omelettes.

TOFU

When Buddhism discouraged meat, it popularized the soy bean, a vegetable protein. Making soybean cake became an art. Buddhist temples vied with one another to develop the perfect soybean cake or *tofu* ("toh-foo"). Served hot or cold, as food or drink, salted or sweet—Japanese food would not be the same without it. The two most common varieties of *tofu* are *kinu-dofu* ("silken *tofu*"), a soft type; and *momen-dofu* ("cotton *tofu*"), a firmer type. One popular dish is the "soybean steak"—a fried *tofu* cake with a thick sweet soy sauce topped with fried fish shavings.

FROM SHABU-SHABU TO SAKE

SHABU-SHABU AND SOY-SAUCE STEWS The universal stew, so welcome when one comes in from the winter cold, is also found in Japan. Many Japanese stews are flavored with soy sauce. They call these stews *nimono* ("nee-moh-noh"). There are hundreds, all as delicious as Chinese claypots and French coq-au-vin. There is also the Japanese version of fondue called *shabu-shabu* ("shah-boo shah-boo"), a word without literal meaning, but one which conveys the sound of bubbling soup in which one dips and cooks a selection of raw meats and vegetables.

TEMPURA *Tempura* ("tam-poo-rah") is prawns, fish, and eggplant and other vegetables dipped in batter and deep fried. The Japanese learned it from the Portuguese and incorporated into their food vocabulary the Portuguese word *tempora* (temporary thing). The Roman Catholic Portuguese could not eat meat on Fridays, so they called the fish-fried-in-batter dish a "temporary thing."

PICKLES Japanese tastes are generally subtle, so sharp stimulants are provided in a variety of pickles called *tsukemono* ("tzoo-kay-moh-noh"). Pickled radish and cucumber—crisp, biting, just a little pungent and sour—add the finishing touch to a meal. Even the herbs and spicy tubers are subtle and play an important role in Japanese cuisine.

SWEETS Japanese make crystallized fruit and spun sugar sweets as the English do, but not the Chinese range of hot sweets. Soy beans form the base of many Japanese sweets. The best flour dumplings are ones with a sweet soybean filling.

Presentation is important; sweets are made in unique shapes and forms, and sold in distinctive packaging. It is one more example of how the visual arts permeate Japanese society.

TEA AND *SAKE* Tea is the drink of Japan. It is offered to the visitor and served at all meals. The Japanese use the honorific O in front of the word *tea* and always refer to tea as *O-cha* ("oh-chah"). The living room of a house is called the *cha-no-ma* ("chah-noh-mah"), the tearoom. Many hundreds of years ago, a formal ceremony for the preparation and offering of tea to special guests was developed; today, it is regarded as an art form.

Sake is the main alcoholic drink. It is made from rice wine and usually drunk warm, although some rare types of *sake* are drunk chilled. Today, cold *sake* is a new fad. A sweetened *sake, mirin* ("mee-rin"), is used for cooking. Special varieties include *amazake* ("ah-mah-zah-kay"), a sweet *sake,* and another with the fin of the puffer fish (blowfish) in it.

Japanese women clad in traditional attire eat special sweets prior to drinking the *matcha* (maht-chah) tea at a formal tea ceremony gathering.

129

MISO SOUP

Most ingredients can be found in the International Foods aisle at your supermarket.
Ingredients:
5 cups water
1 teaspoon of instant *dashi*. Homemade dashi can be made if the ingredients are available
from a 3" x 3" piece of *konbu* (1 ounce of giant kelp *konbu*) and 3 tablespoons of dried
shaved bonito flakes *katsuo-bushi*.
6-8 dried *shiitake* mushrooms
3-4 tablespoons *aka miso* or "red soy bean paste." Miso comes in a variety of flavors,
textures and colors. Generally, white types are sweet, red types are salty.
1/2 pkg. of fresh *tofu*, cut into 1-inch (2.5-cm) squares
3 scallions, chopped

In a medium saucepan combine water and instant *dashi*. Heat over low heat. Meanwhile,
soak dried *shiitake* mushrooms in warm water until tender and rinse out excess water from
mushrooms. (For homemade *dashi*: wipe excess powder off kelp, add to water and bring
to a boil. As water begins to boil add *katsuo-bushi* and lower heat to medium. Remove *konbu*
and *katsuo-bushi* from water.) Cut out and discard mushroom stems. Slice tops thin. Add
to water, bring to a boil. Slowly add *miso* paste by diluting it in water and making sure that
no lumps of paste are left. Reduce heat, add *tofu*, and simmer for a few minutes. Top with
fresh cut scallions and serve. Makes five servings.

TERIYAKI CHICKEN BOWL

Ingredients:
3 pounds chicken breast
Water for boiling chicken breast
1/2 cup soy sauce
1/2 cup brown sugar
1/2 cup ketchup
3 tablespoons honey
1 teaspoon garlic salt
2 teaspoons grated ginger root
Bite-size pieces of broccoli, carrot, cauliflower (steamed)

Boil chicken breast in large covered pot over low heat for 20 minutes. Drain. Combine rest of ingredients and marinate chicken breast in the mixture overnight. Leave a few tablespoons of the mixture aside. Grill chicken breast over charcoal or under the broiler until nicely browned—be careful, for it browns quickly. Cut chicken breast into 2-inch- long strips and serve over a bowl of rice along with steamed vegetables. Warm up leftover teriyaki mixture on a fry pan quickly until the mixture starts to thicken. Pour mixture over chicken and vegetables.

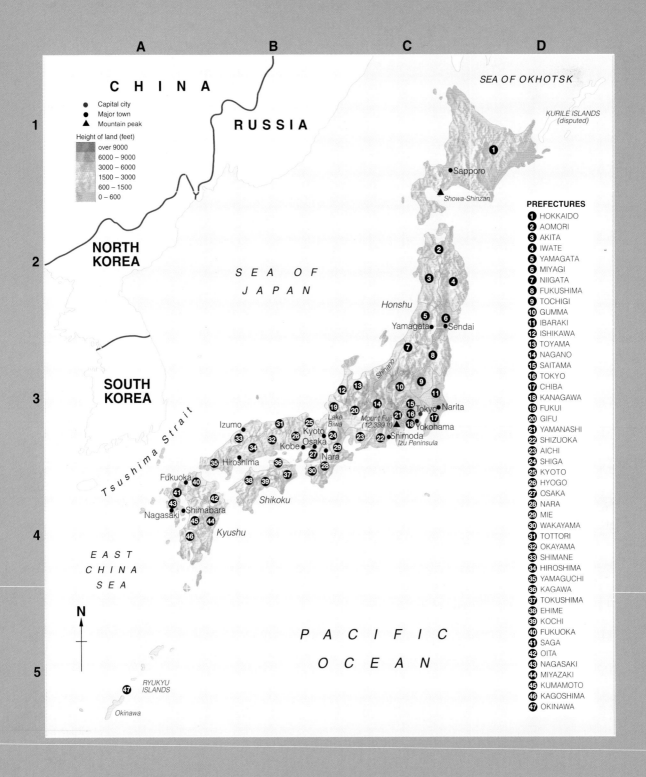

CHINA

RUSSIA

- ● Capital city
- ● Major town
- ▲ Mountain peak

Height of land (feet)
- over 9000
- 6000 – 9000
- 3000 – 6000
- 1500 – 3000
- 600 – 1500
- 0 – 600

NORTH KOREA

SOUTH KOREA

Tsushima Strait

SEA OF JAPAN

Honshu

Yamagata● ●Sendai

Shinano

Tokyo● ●Narita
●Yokohama
●Shimoda
Izu Peninsula

Izumo●

Kyoto ●Lake Biwa
Osaka● ●Nara
Kobe●
Hiroshima●

Fukuoka●
Shimabara●
Nagasaki●

Shikoku

Kyushu

EAST CHINA SEA

N

RYUKYU ISLANDS
Okinawa

PACIFIC OCEAN

SEA OF OKHOTSK

KURILE ISLANDS (disputed)

●Sapporo
▲ *Showa-Shinzan*

Mount Fuji (12,389 ft) ▲

PREFECTURES
1 HOKKAIDO
2 AOMORI
3 AKITA
4 IWATE
5 YAMAGATA
6 MIYAGI
7 NIIGATA
8 FUKUSHIMA
9 TOCHIGI
10 GUMMA
11 IBARAKI
12 ISHIKAWA
13 TOYAMA
14 NAGANO
15 SAITAMA
16 TOKYO
17 CHIBA
18 KANAGAWA
19 FUKUI
20 GIFU
21 YAMANASHI
22 SHIZUOKA
23 AICHI
24 SHIGA
25 KYOTO
26 HYOGO
27 OSAKA
28 NARA
29 MIE
30 WAKAYAMA
31 TOTTORI
32 OKAYAMA
33 SHIMANE
34 HIROSHIMA
35 YAMAGUCHI
36 KAGAWA
37 TOKUSHIMA
38 EHIME
39 KOCHI
40 FUKUOKA
41 SAGA
42 OITA
43 NAGASAKI
44 MIYAZAKI
45 KUMAMOTO
46 KAGOSHIMA
47 OKINAWA

MAP OF JAPAN

Aichi, C3
Akita, C2
Aomori, C2

Chiba, C3
China, A1, A2, B1

East China Sea, A4
Ehime, B4

Fukui, B3–C3
Fukuoka, A3
Fukuoka (city), A4
Fukushima, C3

Gifu, C3
Gumma, C3

Hiroshima, B3
Hiroshima (city), C3
Hokkaido, C1–C2, D1– D2
Honshu, B2–C4
Hyogo, B3

Ibaraki, C3
Ishikawa, C3
Iwate, C2
Izu Peninsula, C3
Izumo, B3

Kagawa, B3–B4
Kagoshima, A4–B4
Kanagawa, C3
Kobe, B3
Kochi, B4
Kumamoto, A4–B4
Kurile Islands, D1
Kyoto, B3
Kyushu, A4–B4

Lake Biwa, B3

Mie, B3–C3
Mount Fuji, C3
Miyagi, C2
Miyazaki, B4

Nagano, C3
Nagasaki, A4
Nagasaki City, A4
Nara, B3–C4
Nara (city), B3
Narita, C3
Niigata, C2–C3
North Korea, A2, A3

Oita, B4
Okayama, B3
Okinawa, A5
Osaka, B3
Osaka (city), B3

Pacific Ocean, B5–D5

Russia, B1
Ryukyu Islands, A5

Saga, A4
Saitama, C3
Sapporo, C1
Sea of Japan, B2
Sea of Okhotsk, D1
Sendai, C2–C3
Shiga, B3
Shikoku, B4
Shimane, B3
Shimoda, C3
Shimabara, A4
Shinano River, C3
Shizuoka, C3

Showa-Shinzan, C1–C2
South Korea, A3

Tochigi, C3
Tokyo, C3
Tokushima, B4
Tottori, B3
Toyama, C3
Tsushima Strait, A3–A4, B3

Wakayama, B4–C4

Yamagata, C2–C3
Yamagata (city), C2
Yamaguchi, B3–B4
Yamanashi, C3
Yokohama, C3

ECONOMIC JAPAN

Agriculture

- Rice
- Poultry
- Fruit
- Vegetables
- Dairy Products

Natural Resources

- Hydroelectricity
- Nuclear Reactor
- Fishing

Manufacturing

- Steel
- Vehicles
- Traditional Arts and Crafts
- Textiles

SEA OF OKHOTSK

Hokkaido

Sapporo

Honshu

Sendai

Yamagata

SEA OF JAPAN

Shinano

TOKYO

Mount Fuji

Narita

Yokohama

Shizuoka

Lake Biwa

Kyoto

Nara

Kobe

Osaka

Izumo

Hiroshima

Fukuoka

Shimahara

Nagasaki

Tsushima Strait

Shikoku

Kyushu

EAST CHINA SEA

PACIFIC OCEAN

ABOUT
THE ECONOMY

OVERVIEW

Japan's industrialized economy is the second largest in the world. It is the world's largest foreign aid donor, a major source of world capital, and a technology leader in many fields. With limited natural resources, however, Japan is highly dependent on imported raw materials, such as petroleum, iron, and aluminum ores.

GDP

US$4.356 trillion (1999)

GDP SECTORS

Agriculture: 2%
Industry: 35%
Services: 63%

LAND USE

Arable Land: 13%
Permanent Crops: 1%
Permanent Pastures: 2%
Forests and Woodland: 67%
Others: 8% (1997 est.)
Irrigated Land: 17,276 sq miles (44,745 square km) (1993 est.)

CURRENCY

1 Yen = 100 sen
Notes: 1,000, 2,000, 5,000, and 10,000 yen
Coins: 1, 5, 10, 50, 100, and 500 yen
US$1 = 110 yen (Dec 2000)

WORKFORCE

67.79 million (1999)
Trade and Services: 65%
Industry: 30%
Agriculture, forestry, and fishing: 5%

AGRICULTURAL PRODUCTS

Rice, sugar beets, vegetables, fruit, pork, poultry, dairy products, eggs, fish

MAJOR EXPORTS

Automobiles, iron and steel, video cassette recorders, office equipment, scientific and optical equipment, ships, prime movers, metal products, radio receivers, metalworking machinery

MAJOR IMPORTS

Food, raw materials, mineral fuels, chemicals, textiles, machinery and equipment

MAJOR TRADING PARTNERS

United States, Taiwan, China, South Korea
Hong Kong, Australia (1999)

UNEMPLOYMENT RATE

4.6% (2000)

HIGHWAYS

715,981 miles (1,152,000 km) (1999 est.)

RAILROADS

17,028 miles (27,404 km) (1997)

WATERWAYS

Approx. 1,100 miles (1,770 km)

CULTURAL JAPAN

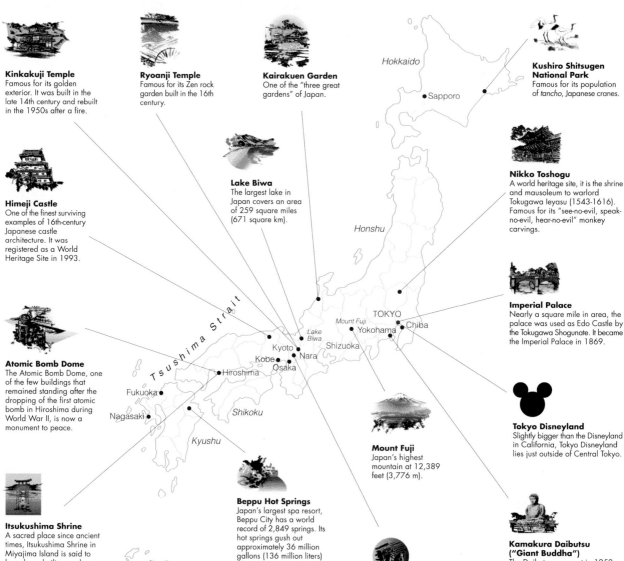

Kinkakuji Temple
Famous for its golden exterior. It was built in the late 14th century and rebuilt in the 1950s after a fire.

Ryoanji Temple
Famous for its Zen rock garden built in the 16th century.

Kairakuen Garden
One of the "three great gardens" of Japan.

Kushiro Shitsugen National Park
Famous for its population of *tancho*, Japanese cranes.

Himeji Castle
One of the finest surviving examples of 16th-century Japanese castle architecture. It was registered as a World Heritage Site in 1993.

Lake Biwa
The largest lake in Japan covers an area of 259 square miles (671 square km).

Nikko Toshogu
A world heritage site, it is the shrine and mausoleum to warlord Tokugawa Ieyasu (1543-1616). Famous for its "see-no-evil, speak-no-evil, hear-no-evil" monkey carvings.

Atomic Bomb Dome
The Atomic Bomb Dome, one of the few buildings that remained standing after the dropping of the first atomic bomb in Hiroshima during World War II, is now a monument to peace.

Imperial Palace
Nearly a square mile in area, the palace was used as Edo Castle by the Tokugawa Shogunate. It became the Imperial Palace in 1869.

Tokyo Disneyland
Slightly bigger than the Disneyland in California, Tokyo Disneyland lies just outside of Central Tokyo.

Mount Fuji
Japan's highest mountain at 12,389 feet (3,776 m).

Itsukushima Shrine
A sacred place since ancient times, Itsukushima Shrine in Miyajima Island is said to have been built as early as A.D. 593.

Beppu Hot Springs
Japan's largest spa resort, Beppu City has a world record of 2,849 springs. Its hot springs gush out approximately 36 million gallons (136 million liters) of spring water every day.

Kamakura Daibutsu ("Giant Buddha")
The Daibutsu was cast in 1252. Over 36 feet (11 m) tall and 95 feet (29 m) at the base, the statue is cast in bronze and is estimated to weigh at least 90 tons.

Shuri Castle
Reconstructed castle of the ancient Ryukyu kingdom. The original structure was destroyed during World War II.

Horyuji
A World Heritage Site, the present Buddhist temple was built between A.D. 670 and 714.

Hokkaido

Sapporo

Honshu

TOKYO

Lake Biwa

Mount Fuji

Yokohama

Chiba

Shizuoka

Kyoto

Nara

Kobe

Osaka

Hiroshima

Fukuoka

Nagasaki

Shikoku

Kyushu

Tsushima Strait

ABOUT
THE CULTURE

OFFICIAL NAME
Japan

CAPITAL
Tokyo

DESCRIPTION OF FLAG
White background with a red disk in the center

POPULATION
126.7 million (Jan 2000)

ETHNIC GROUPS
Japanese 99.4%, Others (mostly Koreans) 0.6%

LIFE EXPECTANCY
Male 77, female 84 (1998)

NATIONAL ANTHEM
Kimigayo ("The Reign of Our Emperor")

TIME
Greenwich Mean Time plus 9 hours (GMT +0900)

LITERACY RATE
99 percent

LEADERS IN SPORTS
Tokyo Giants baseball legends, Nagashima Shigeo and Oh Sadaharu; Nomo Hideo, baseball player, currently playing for the Boston Red Sox in the United States; Nakata Hidetoshi, soccer player, currently playing for A. S. Roma in Italy.

LEADERS IN LITERATURE
Natsume Soseki, Kawabata Yasunari, Mishima Yukio, Oe Kenzaburo, Murakami Haruki

NATIONAL HOLIDAYS
New Year's Day (Jan. 1), Coming of Age Day (Jan. 15*), National Foundation Day (Feb. 11*), Vernal Equinox (Mar. 20*), Greenery Day (Apr. 29), Constitution Day (May 3), National Holiday (May 4), Children's Day (May 5), Marine Day (Jul. 20), Respect for the Aged Day (Sep. 15), Autumnal Equinox (Sep. 23), Health Sports Day (Oct. 8), Culture Day (Nov. 3), Labor Thanksgiving Day (Nov. 23), and the Emperor's Birthday (Dec. 23). *From 2001, this day may be moved to either the Friday of the previous week or the Monday of the following week.

SYSTEM OF GOVERNMENT
Constitutional monarchy with a parliamentary government.

WORKING LIFE
Japanese, on average, work 40 hours a week (eight hours a day) and enjoy ten days of vacation a year. Some companies work half day on Saturday.

IN JAPAN	IN THE WORLD
	753 B.C. Rome founded
	116–17 B.C. Roman Empire reaches its greatest extent, under Emperor Trajan (98-17)
538–552 Buddhism is introduced to Japan	**600 A.D.** Height of Mayan civilization
645 The Taika Reform begins, and sets up central government controlled by the emperor	
710 The first capital is established in Nara	
794 The capital is moved to Heian—present-day Kyoto. (Heian period 794–1185)	
	1000 Chinese perfect gunpowder and begin to use it in warfare
1192 Kamakura military government is established	
1334 Emperor regains power over Japan	
	1530 Beginning of trans-Atlantic slave trade organized by Portuguese in Africa
1542 Portuguese missionaries arrive in Japan	**1558–1603** Reign of Elizabeth I of England
1600 Victory of Tokugawa Ieyasu at Battle of Sekigahara	
1603 Tokugawa Ieyasu establishes the Tokugawa military government in Edo (present-day Tokyo)	

IN JAPAN	IN THE WORLD
	1620 Pilgrim Fathers sail the Mayflower to America
1639 *Sakoku* policy begins, isolating Japan almost completely from the rest of the world	
	1776 U. S. Declaration of Independence
	1789–1799 The French Revolution
1854 Japan opens up for trade with the West	**1861** U. S. Civil War begins
1868 The Meiji Restoration takes place	**1869** The Suez Canal is opened
1914–18 Japan joins Allied Forces in World War I	**1914** World War I begins
1937 Second Sino-Japanese War begins	
1941 War in the Pacific starts	**1939** World War II begins
1945 Two atomic bombs are dropped over Hiroshima and Nagasaki. Japan surrenders	**1945** The United States drops atomic bombs on Hiroshima and Nagasaki
	1949 North Atlantic Treaty Organization (NATO) formed
1952 Allied Occupation of Japan ends	
1956 Japan joins the United Nations	**1957** Russians launch Sputnik
1964 Japan hosts the Olympic Games in Tokyo	**1966–1969** Chinese Cultural Revolution
	1986 Nuclear power disaster at Chernobyl in Ukraine
1993 Thirty-eight-year rule by Liberal Democratic Party ends	**1991** Break-up of Soviet Union
1995 Great Hanshin-Awaji earthquake hits the city of Kobe	**1997** Hong Kong is returned to China
	2001 World population surpasses 6 billion

GLOSSARY

Ainu
Aboriginal people of Japan, now mainly confined to the northern island of Hokkaido.

bonsai ("bon-zye")
Japanese traditional art of growing miniature potted trees

daimyo ("dye-mee-yoh")
Feudal chieftain of old Japan

haiku ("hie-koo")
Traditional Japanese short poem consisting of 5-7-5 syllables

ikebana ("ee-kay-bah-nah")
Japanese traditional art of flower arrangement

juku ("joo-koo")
Japanese cram schools

kabuki ("kah-boo-key")
Japanese traditional theater which combines acting, singing accompaniment, and dancing.

kana ("kah-nah")
Japanese phonetic script

kanji ("kan-jee")
Chinese characters used in the Japanese writing system today

kimono ("key-moh-noh")
Japanese one-piece wraparound garment held together by an *obi* sash

matsuri ("maht-soo-ree")
Festival

miso ("mee-soh")
Rich, savory paste of malt, salt, and fermented soy beans used in Japanese cooking.

sake ("sah-kay")
Japanese rice wine

samurai ("sah-moo-rye")
Japanese warrior of historical times

sempai-kohai ("sam-pie koh-high")
The relationship between a senior and a junior at school, work, and clubs, on sports teams, and in Japanese society in general

seppuku ("sep-poo-koo")
Ritual suicide by slitting one's own belly with a sword. The more common (vulgar) term is *harakiri*.

shogun ("show-goon")
Military ruler of Japan

sushi ("soo-shee")
A small piece of fresh fish on bite-size lumps of rice seasoned with vinegar

tofu ("toh-foo")
A soft or firm curd made from soy beans that is a rich source of protein.

torii ("toh-ree-ee")
Gateway to a Shinto shrine

FURTHER INFORMATION

BOOKS

Fodor's Japan. Expert Advice and Smart Choices: Where to Stay, Eat, and Explore On and Off the Beaten Path. 15th ed. New York: Fodor's Travel Publications, 2000.

Haugaard, Erik Christian. *The Revenge of the Forty-Seven Samurai*. Boston: Houghton Miffin Co. (Juv.), 1995.

Netzley, Patricia D. *Japan (Modern Nations of the World)*. San Diego: Lucent Books, 2000.

Reiber, Beth, et al. *Frommer's Japan*. 5th ed. New York: Hungry Minds, 2000.

Rowthorn, Chris, et al. *Lonely Planet Japan*. 7th ed. London: Lonely Planet Publications, 2000.

Yoshikawa, Eiji; translated by William Scott Wilson. *Taiko: An Epic Novel of War and Glory in Feudal Japan*. Tokyo: Kodansha International, 2001.

WEBSITES

Central Intelligence Agency World Factbook (select Japan from the country list).
www.odci.gov/cia/publications/factbook/index.html

Cleveland State University's website on Japan has numerous links devoted to aspects of Japanese culture and civilization. www.csuohio.edu/history/japan/

Japan Computer Access Network and the Association for Progressive Communication website encourages the participation of Japanese citizens in different social activities through the Internet. www.jca.apc.org/index-en.html

Japan Defense Agency. www.jda.go.jp/e/index_.htm

Japan Information Network. www.jinjapan.org

Japan National Tourist Organization. www.jnto.go.jp

Learning Network reference (type "Japan" in the search box). http://ln.infoplease.com

U.S. Department of State webpage on Japan.
www.state.go/www/background_notes/japan_0007_bgn.html

The World Bank Group (type "Japan" in the search box). www.worldbank.org

VIDEOS

Great Cultures Great Nations, Japan: The Land of the Rising Sun. London: Madacy Entertainment, 1997.

BIBLIOGRAPHY

Beasley, W.G. *The Modern History of Japan* (Third Revised Edition). Tokyo: Charles E. Tuttle Company, Inc., 1992.

Discover Japan (Volumes 1 & 2). New York: Kodansha International, USA Limited, 1986.

Hall, John Whitney. Japan—From Prehistory to Modern Times. Tokyo: Charles E. Tuttle Company, Inc., 1992.

JETRO (Ed.). *Nippon 2000 — Business Facts and Figures.* Tokyo: Japan External Trade Organization (JETRO), 2000.

Ministry of Finance (Ed.). *Japan Statistical Yearbook 2000* (49th Ed.). Japan: Statistics Bureau Management and Coordination Agency, Ministry of Finance, 2000.

INDEX